Fastpitch.tv
NETWORK
PRESENTS

The Fastpitch Book

20 GREAT COACHES
GIVE YOU 20 GREAT TOOLS
TO IMPROVE YOUR GAME

WWW.FASTPITCHBOOK.COM

The Fastpitch Book

20 Great Coaches Give You
20 Great Tools
To Improve Your Game

Complied By Gary Leland

ISBN-13: 9781514817605

ISBN-10: 1514817608

Printed in the United States of America

Table of Contents

4

Preface

I want to thank you for purchasing this book, and I hope the advice and knowledge shared in its contents will help you in your fastpitch softball career. I reached out to my personal contacts list of coaches and asked each of them to submit their advice from their combined years of experience in fastpitch softball.

This book was then compiled of 20 of the best articles written by 20 great fastpitch softball coaches from around the nation. It also includes several bonus tips from many other professional coaches. This information is meant to give insight and thought processes in the game of fastpitch softball. Many tools and techniques behind what it takes to build a successful team.

Good luck reaching for your next championship!

Aaron Weintraub

"Mental Toughness Stems from a Healthy Perspective"

"Softball is what I do, not who I am."

"I might get beat, but I'll never be defeated!"

"Softball is not war. I compete fiercely, but it is just a game."

"I love this game."

- Why does one person break down under pressure while another breaks through?
- How can an athlete perform so well in practice, and then struggle so mightily in the game?
- Why do many fine athletes work hard and have talent, but play so inconsistently?

Many coachable, hard-working athletes perform far below their potential because they are unaware of their deficient mental skills. With awareness, many mental skills can be trained such as focus, self-control, imagery, and confidence. All are parts of the answers to the questions above, but none address a foundational problem found in most inconsistent athletes' mental game: a flawed perspective.

If a competitor does not win, does that make her a loser? Absolutely not, but socialization into America's competitive, capitalist culture teaches many elite athletes to *feel* this way. Our culture promotes the *false* idea that winning on the scoreboard is all that matters. The idea that value depends on achievement is a distorted belief. A person's worth does not fluctuate based on today's performance on the diamond. All humans have inalienable rights; our value is immeasurable and it cannot diminish. A healthy perspective on success defines that word in controllable terms. The idea that success depends on achievement is also a distorted belief. It is an extremely common belief, but it is false. Achievement is a logical by-product of success, but sometimes logic is bypassed because of factors outside of the person's control.

Perspective is the, "ability to see things in a true relationship" to one another. It can also mean "a specific point of view in understanding things or events". Top athletes explain life to themselves honestly. They also look at the truth in a manner that is useful. A healthy perspective allows athletes to improve faster, lead effectively, and perform well through adversity and pressure. Honesty is critical because they will not be able to lie to themselves. Finding a useful angle with which to view the truth is also critical. There are two sides to every coin. While both sides are real (true), only one is most useful for creating confidence, an ideal internal state, and maximizing productivity. For example, a 12-ounce cup with six ounces of water in it can accurately be called half full or half empty. It is most useful, assuming you are thirsty, to view it as half full.

The first step to a healthy perspective on softball is to recognize that it *is* just a game. Sports pose no life-or-death propositions. Parents will not stop loving because of what happens in the third inning. Athletes in "big" moments on television may have literally millions of eyes on them and be "tough" enough to perform with total freedom. Many kids in youth leagues seem to carry the weight of the world on their shoulders. The source of these polar opposites is not the situation, but the way the athletes perceive the situation. A healthy perspective empowers competitors to be free from worry, which in turn allows them to get totally engrossed in the moment. When an athlete is engrossed in the moment, she is powerful. She is slowing the game down and focusing with tunnel vision on the task at hand. It makes sense: to focus effectively, it is necessary to look at things the right way!

An attitude of gratitude is a foundational piece of a healthy perspective. Being thankful improves the heart's rhythmic functioning, which reduces stress, promotes clarity of thought, and aids the healing process. It is physiologically impossible to feel stressful and grateful at the same time. Grateful athletes are more relaxed, more coachable, more forgiving, more present to the task at hand, and generally more positive than their counterparts. They are less likely to complain. Author Jon Gordon says, "Remember that complaining is like vomiting. Afterwards you feel better but everyone around you feels sick." Champions live out the words of John Wooden, "Don't whine. Don't complain. Don't make excuses." They are consistently grateful.

"I won the lottery when I was born."

Athletes love to be "in rhythm;" this is more likely to happen when they are "in gratitude." Winning the lottery means gaining immense wealth at odds of perhaps 10,000,000 or more to 1. America has some real problems, without a doubt, but when compared to all the present and past times and places to be born, living in 21st century America is quite a blessing. The odds of landing somewhere with this many opportunities for health, wealth, freedom, happiness, contribution, and satisfaction are, statistically speaking, much greater than the odds of winning the lottery!

An ideal perspective for performance recognizes that "who I am *is important*." How things go in competition today will certainly impact how

9

much fun is had. It may also impact things like material possessions and reputation. These are important, too, but not nearly as important as the reputation the athlete acquires with herself. Great athletes refuse to be in an adversarial relationship with themselves, and they have integrity. They think, speak, and act in comfortable alignment with their personal values.

Performance outcomes do matter for many reasons. Besides affecting enjoyment, they provide feedback. Outcomes reveal the truth about what works. However, no single outcome should ever be given too much importance. No loss should ever be seen as a catastrophe. No "failure" should be allowed to carry an emotional scar of inadequacy. Fear of "failure," which everyone has to some degree, does not interfere with performance if the athlete has a healthy perspective. She can be scared, but act courageously because she believes that by putting forth great effort, she cannot fail. Her success is inevitable because she designs, practices, and executes her plans (a.k.a. performance routines) to the best of her ability. She defines success like John Wooden did in 1934: "The peace of mind that comes from knowing you did your best."

Winning begins now!

The idea that game days are more important than other days is a dangerous way to look at competition. John Wooden won a National Championship as a player and 10 more in his final 12 years as a basketball coach at UCLA. His father taught him to count his blessings and make *each* day his masterpiece. The father of football coaches John and Jim Harbaugh (the opposing head coaches in the 2013 Super Bowl) taught them to "attack this day with enthusiasm unknown to mankind." Today is all an athlete can control, and it is exactly when approaching potential happens.

Athletes who handle pressure well use their excitement to enhance performance rather than allow their nerves to detract from it. They care about their performance in practice as much (or—being realistic—almost as much) as their performance in competition. American society leads the other way. Since practice outcomes do not have as many ramifications as game outcomes, the prevailing attitude is that it is okay to take a "do-over" in practice, even though no do-overs exist in competition. Certainly, more practice is appropriate when mistakes are being made, but the next one does not *make up* for a mistake on the last one. There are no do-overs in life.

To get closer to the goal of caring as much about practice as games, the most useful perspective puts approaching potential at the top of the healthy athlete's goals. Achieving this goal through steady discipline provides peace of mind *and* maximizes chances to get all the rewards that normally define success: championships, scholarships, recognition, etc. The rewards that most people think define success are actually a by-product of the goal, not the goal itself. The essence of success is continual improvement. Best effort now is all an athlete can do. It is never achieved easily; it requires hard and smart work. A champion appreciates that the only *time* she can control that affects approaching potential is *right now*. An athlete wins the mental side of the game when she gives her best effort now, accept whatever happens, and then repeats this process. Champions are intense people. The importance of now raises her intensity level throughout practice, which allows the "clutch" situation to feel similar to her. She is, as much as is possible, comfortable being uncomfortable.

A winner's attitude towards a "clutch" moment in competition is impressive. She views every performance as an opportunity to evaluate and display all of her preparation. Others may focus on the pressure, but she knows that increased pressure is the shadow of increased opportunity. This opportunity is her chance to "show off" to herself (especially), her family, her teammates, and others the combination of her talents and her industriousness. The bigger stage is the better stage, as far as she is concerned, because she has earned the right to be proud and confident. In fact, she lives for that big moment that follows the thought, "Bring it on! I know I will succeed because I know I will execute the plans I have designed to give my best effort one pitch at a time."

Winning is far better than the alternative, but the "winning is everything" perspective is a problem because it does not encourage effort if the victory can be obtained easily. It also does not encourage effort if maximum effort is not perceived to be likely to lead to winning. In fact, it (often subconsciously) discourages it because the person who loses without maximum effort can still defend her win-driven ego by believing that if she had tried harder, she *might* have won. However, if she took the chance of giving maximum effort and did not get the desired outcome, she would have no solace. She would feel like a "failure." Not giving her best effort is not only easier, it is also perceived to be safer. Many athletes keep this "safety net" for their psyche. Great competitors do not know what will happen, but because of their perspective on success, they do not fear the unknown. They do not need a safety net.

Every athlete experiences many challenges and setbacks along the journey to find out how good she can be. Fortunately, no softball player has to travel this path alone. In fact, a winner knows that trying to be the best she can be by herself is fruitless. Together Everyone Achieves More, so an athlete with a healthy perspective is also a leader who appreciates her teammates. She not only works hard and has a consistently positive attitude; she also goes out of her way to help others. She admires those who excel, rather than criticizing them. In fact, she has a personal rule against criticizing a teammate in public. She has no interest in competing with her own teammates. Rather, she encourages and compliments them. She is patient with those who struggle, knowing that she, too, has weaknesses. Everyone's strengths and weaknesses are different. She is encouraging and optimistic when times are tough and comfortable expressing joy and appreciation when times are good. Her teammates love having her around.

A healthy perspective encourages this leader to get better fast by thinking like a scientist. She is racing to perform her best and she views each obstacle as a stepping-stone. Winners compete, with themselves first and foremost, but they do not worry about losing. Challenges and pitfalls provide motivation for them to get better; they are not viewed as disappointments or "failures." A scientist just wants to find out which things work and which things could be done better. Outcomes are no longer bad or good, they are always both. Emotions stay on an even keel. Adversity provides an opportunity to both learn and practice avoiding the negative snowball effect. Champions use mistakes constructively rather than letting them snowball into a "slump." Plus, skill will not improve as quick if the athlete does not push the limits of her own familiar zone (often called a comfort zone). Yes, mistakes are good. Because of a healthy perspective, the athlete improves at asking and answering the ultimate questions:

"Where am I?"

"Where do I want to go?"

And, *"How do I get there?"*

"Who are you competing with this weekend?" The best answer is "myself." In a big game, a mentally tough athletes confidence is doubled by her superb mental skills and that of her teammates. She is doubtful that her opponents have such a healthy perspective on the game or that they are as thoroughly prepared as she and her team, both physically and mentally. The ironic truth is that the person who wants to produce positive outcomes because she defines her success by her achievement is much less likely than the person with a healthy perspective to get that good outcome. So it is: trying to win by outscoring the other team decreases the chance of that happening; trying to win versus oneself increases the chance of winning on the scoreboard. The athlete with the flawed perspective does not know if she will be comfortable looking at herself in the mirror after the game. The healthy athlete knows.

B.E. = A.G.E.
Best Effort is Always Good Enough!

Aaron Weintraub

Aaron holds a B.A. from Emory University (1993) and a M.Ed. from the University of Virginia (2000). He coached college baseball from 1994-2006. In 2006, he started www.CoachTraub.com, a consulting business whose mission is to over-deliver value on goods and services designed to help you and yours W.I.N. the mental side of the game. He works with teams and individuals, adding clarity to help them get what they want from their sport. CoachTraub.com also runs camps and clinics and has an online store. Weintraub started www.SmileNowCoach.com in 2014, a blog with motivational and educational resources for coaches.

Weintraub is the author of Coaches Guide to Winning the Mental Game (Coaches Choice, 2009), Leadership Training for Softball (2nd Edition - 2014), and Leadership Training for Baseball (2015). He has spoken at local and national coaching conventions and worked with softball teams at all levels, including Ole Miss, Georgia Tech, UCF, Arizona, NMSU, UTA, and McNeese St.

Bryan Burrows Ingalis

"A New Approach to Catcher Training"

The game of softball is getting faster, more athletic, more intellectual. Gone are the days of putting the un-athletic kid behind the plate to take up space. Even in the past few years we have seen catchers become more athletic; we have seen schools and colleges converting shortstops and center fielders into catchers due to the importance of arm strength, speed, and agility.

Recently a study was done saying the walks are way up in college softball. They try to say that pitching has gone down and is not at the level it used to be. I disagree. Pitching is just as good as or better than it was even 5 years ago. More pitchers are touching 70 MPH than ever before and moving the ball very well. What I do see a difference is in coaching. The coaching profession has gotten so much better and there are so many great approaches to hitting. Great college softball players have taken a love for coaching and many former men's fastpitch players have gotten involved in the women's game and together that has made the game of fastpitch softball more popular than ever.

There are so many new and efficient hitting and pitching drills. Great baseball instructors are coming in and relating to the game of softball, which has helped create better contact and power. These men's fastpitch pitchers are throwing batting practice to their team's everyday so the days of 65 MPH being a speed that hitters cannot handle is long gone. Everything evolves, but what will always to an ace in the hole is a 5-tool catcher.

Having a 5-tool catcher is something that every coach should try to look for and/or develop; but they are not the typical 5 tools that are sought out in a normal softball player. Offense has nothing to do with being a 5-tool catcher and neither does blocking, believe it or not.

My 5 tools to be a top of the line catcher are as follows: stealing strikes (and not taking them away), pitch calling, keeping the bad pitches in front, communicating with the defense, and being a confidant for the pitchers. These are 5 things that inevitably make the pitchers the most comfortable. It does not matter what the capability of the pitcher is if they are not confident in and comfortable with the person receiving their pitches. The catcher can and will directly affect how the pitcher throws that game, inning, and pitch and it is their job to get the best performance out of their pitcher.

Strike zones are seemingly getting smaller as our pitchers continue to get better. Catchers need to spend more time learning how to steal strikes. This is not just framing good pitches, but taking balls and bringing them back into the strike zone, especially drop balls. Rise balls are something that every pitcher wants to throw and it gets a lot of swing and misses, but great hitters are learning how to lay off of them and or learning how to hit them. Close misses with rise balls are easy homeruns and big hitters take advantage of that. Well-placed drop balls are ground balls and ground balls are typically outs. What we have to do as catchers is steal those drop balls for strikes so that the hitters are forced to swing at those pitches with 2 strikes. Just like balls off of the plate, we have to attack the pitch from the outside of the strike zone and work in. This is not a catch and frame, or a catch and snap of the wrist to make it look better. Its an all out attack from the outside of the strike zone and timing the point of catch with the arm locking out is crucial so it's one movement.

Great catchers can steal many inches with their point of attack on balls out of the strike zone. The key is in the set up. If a catcher extends the arm early and away from their body, it will severely hinder this process and may actually make some strikes look like balls. A neutral position and target with the hand and glove close to the body will give you a great chance at attacking these pitches; it will also allow the catcher to move a little bit closer to the plate. Remember every inch counts when stealing strikes. The more strikes you can steal the more comfortable the pitcher feels and we all know how important that is.

The art of calling a game is something that can be taught but a lot of that is developed in the pitcher/catcher relationship. Great pitch callers go on feel and sight of the hitter during the game. Studying and plans of attack can be developed pre game but every day we as players are different. It is crucial to learn pitchers tendencies and figure out what pitches work that day along with what the hitters are bringing to the table. Even the smallest details like the weather, the fielders, and flow of the game are all things that catchers need to take into account when calling their next pitch. Pitch calling can be learned in a classroom, but the best sessions are learned with your battery mate during a game.

One thing that you see a lot of these days are dozens of different blocking drills for catchers. They look great and they really help develop the quickness and the athleticism that is needed this day and age for catchers. What we need to be aware of is not spending entirely too much time with the blocking form and banging up and down with our legs. It's a great workout, yes, but also we need to realize how important our legs are and many of these drills can put a beating on your knees and legs in the long run. The mentality of blocking needs to turn into "keeping the bad pitch in front of us." A common theme is starting to happen in softball:

many catchers are performing correct blocking form, but are not keeping the ball in front of them. Catchers need to learn their range and how far from side to side they can go before they have to just try and reach and grab it. Sometimes keeping it simple and asking yourself what your task was and did I complete it is. When we block, we do want to create a soft barrier and have our hips behind our shoulders with our heads tucked, but what we do not want to do is lose ground in the process. When we do that we give the ball more distance to travel upward so that we use the chest protector, when sometimes we can gain ground and get it on the short hop, and not even have to take the chance of letting it hit something and kick another way. We need to smother the ball and come get it. As a fastpitch catcher who catches around 100 games a year I do not think I have ever had to actually use my chest protector more than 10 times in any given season and a majority of those were on change ups that were in the dirt. What really makes the pitcher confident is not just blocking a ball but also just keeping it in front regardless of what the "form" looks like. Keeping it close in case there is a play to be made, but most importantly having the ability to catch those pitches that are just plain bad misses. If you can take a couple pitches a game that would normally be at the screen and snag them, you become the pitchers hero, but that takes practice. Have someone who can throw the ball but may not actually be a pitcher and just throw the ball hard. It is extremely uncomfortable for a catcher but it will make for a more comfortable pitcher in the long run.

As you become more comfortable with the pitchers and have an idea of what each pitch is doing, you will start to have an idea of where each ball will be hit if hit hard and also hit softly. Help directing the defense from your point of view is something that is absolutely a must. A game that is as quick as this every step is needed! And trust me more than anyone; your corner infielders will truly appreciate it. Putting them in a position to not only make a play but also protect themselves is something that goes a long way with teammates and the overall success of the team. It builds the confidence in you and makes them less hesitant when you direct them to play even closer to home plate to take away a potential bunt or sacrifice play.

The last thing, but also the most important thing that you are as a catcher, is a confidant to your pitching staff. They depend on you to not only guide them in the right direction but pick them up with they are down and keep them grounded when they are rolling. Learning the psychological tendencies of your pitcher will not only help you get more out of them but it will help build that pitcher/catcher relationship, ultimately leading to team success. Learn what makes them go and learn what puts them down. Everything and everyone is different. What may work with one pitcher may not work with another. Some need to be pushed, and others shut down when pushed. Challenge the pitchers in practice, training and, pre game.

This game is mental and the most important piece is the catcher. This position is ever evolving and we must evolve with it. Get faster, get stronger, get smarter and most importantly try your best to keep things simple. Be happy with getting a job done, not necessarily what it looks like. If we worry about what everything looks like, sometimes we end up doing too much and that takes away from our intended job. Efficient movements, positive reinforcement, and communication are what great catchers bring to the table. If you want to be a 5-tool catcher, steal strikes, call a great game, keep the bad pitches in front, communicate with the defense, and be a confidant to your pitchers. If you can do that, you can and will go a long way in this game.

About Bryan Burrows Ingalis

Began coaching Fastpitch Softball at the age of 19 as an assistant for a travel ball program in upstate New York. At the end of his baseball playing days in college at SUNY Cortland, he came across the sport of Men's Fastpitch Softball in the Northern Fastpitch League based out of Prospect, NY. At 21, he began as an assistant Softball coach at Herkimer College and over the pitchers and catchers during his 3rd season. Bryan was at Herkimer for 4 years with their win total increasing every year he was there. His last year there Herkimer led the NJCAA D3 in Team ERA with all 3 of his starting Pitchers individually in the top 10.

After Herkimer, Bryan moved to Cortland to Assist NFCA Hall of Fame Coach Julie Lenhart and that stint was cut short after being offered a Head Coaching Position at SUNY Canton mid-year. After 1 season at Canton Bryan decided to head in another direction and pursue his first passion in opening and running a Multi Sport and Fitness facility and in November 2014 Accelerate Sports opened its door in Whitesboro, NY. He currently instructs out of Accelerate and at various clinics in and out of the region (www.accelerate-sports.com).

Charity Butler

"Confidence Coaching"

Caution to the narrow-minded and the comfortable. Be warned all who refuse and despise change. An unavoidable, permanent shift in perspective lies moments ahead. A revelation awaits all who dare to read on.

Still reading? Good. Let's get started.

Look closely at the logo for the company, FedEx. Google it if you need. Have you ever noticed the hidden arrow in the logo? Look between the "E" and the "X". Aha! Once you have seen the arrow, it is impossible to ever miss again. The logo remains the same, as the arrow was always present. The image did not transform before your eyes. What changed? You did. Your perspective shifted, and now you see what was always there. In a sense, you are looking with new eyes, so you see the exact same logo more completely.

After years of competing, coaching and instructing, I have recently come to realize that it is not accurate enough to call me a softball coach or hitting instructor. Rather, I am a Confidence Coach. While I may spend hours upon hours helping an athlete perfect a skill, it is not time and effort alone that empower an athlete.

The secret to unlocking latent potential and equipping athletes to exceed even their own expectations is in the intrinsic. A shift in perspective is required to understand and practice Confidence Coaching.

Christina Marshall, CEO of Intrinsic Solutions International and Founder of the Intrinsic Coaching® methodology, says this: "In a word, it's math… correct mathematical thinking about people." Trying to fully explain this statement in several paragraphs or even several pages is truly impossible. However, in the movie *The Fault in Our Stars*, Hazel Grace describes the idea quite concisely:

"There are infinite numbers between 0 and 1. There are .1 and .12 and .112 and an infinite collection of others. Of course, there is a bigger infinite set of numbers between 0 and 2, or between 0 and a million. Some infinities are bigger than other infinities."

Christina tabs this concept the Math of Life. Intrinsic math breaks the 1, 2, 3 mold and encompasses the .1's, .12's and .112's of life. Some players thrive under pressure and others implode. Likewise, the same athlete can be MVP of the game today and find herself with confidence shaken tomorrow.

In an effort to understand these seemingly fickle athletes, we label players as "head cases," "cocky," "confident," "gamers" and the like. These stereotypes are analogous to finite numbers (1's, 2's and 3's). If not viewed properly, these categories pigeonhole our thinking and limit our ability to unleash maximum potential.

Getting to the root of any confidence challenge or mental block is not as simple as 1, 2, 3. Answers are found in the .1, .12 and .112 infinities in between, the unpredictable variations and absolute uniqueness of each player.

Consider a question as simple as, "What motivates you?"

The answer provided will be, like finite numbers, limiting. What we think we know and understand is incomplete because we cannot comprehend the under-the-surface, infinite and unique set of experiences that led to this tip-of-the-iceberg answer. Armed with only partial information, we then make inaccurate assumptions. We miss the .1's, .12's and .112's.

Consider the following example:

I was asked by a D1 collegiate coach to hold several Confidence Coaching sessions with one of her pitchers who was struggling with consistency on the mound. For privacy's sake, we will call her Ashley. Ashley's symptoms of inconsistency and lack of confidence were the finite 1's, 2's and 3's.

Through our work together, she realized she cared more about others opinions than her own. She ended a toxic relationship and rekindled her love for pitching all in the same week. With no knowledge of her choices and changes, Ashley's coach commented, "You look like a different person this week." Her pitching performance skyrocketed, her confidence grew and her personal life gained healthier balance.

I had no idea the choices she made or the under-the-surface processing that lead to those realizations. She found her own answers in places I could not touch, the .1's, .12's and .112's of her own life. These are the infinite nuances of the intrinsic domain. She started paying attention to what was important for *her*, and she came up with solutions I could not provide. I gave her the tools to broaden her perspective, but she did the work. She found the solutions on her own, more effectively than I could attempt to do for her.

Ashley is the expert on *her* life; I am not. If I were to make snap judgments based on what I could see on the surface, I would have made completely incorrect assumptions. The intrinsic begins where assumption ends.

Sure, I could have assumed I was the expert. I could have attempted to provide excellent strategies for increasing her consistency. Nonetheless, my suggestions would have been entirely off the mark, counterproductive and absolutely frustrating for her because I am not equipped to give her the answers she really needs. I cannot access her .1's .12's and .112's.

All we can provide others is the 1, 2, 3 kind of advice. When tapping into the intrinsic, though, the infinite .1's, .12's and .112's are all accessible. The solutions are vastly different and ultimately more valuable. Like the FedEx logo, Intrinsic Coaching® unlocks a new perspective and allows us to see what we have been habitually missing.

You have already begun the process by reading this chapter. You are certainly considering the possibility of a fresh perspective… a different approach.

Start exploring the intrinsic by simply committing during practice and training to the following:

i.   Provide necessary instruction.
ii. Allow players to put the new information into practice.
iii. Ask, "What did you feel? What did you notice?"

Be quiet and listen. Give athletes time to think, process and respond. Their answers will surprise you and solutions you cannot create for them will unfold!

About Charity Butler

Charity Butler, CIC®, CVS® is respected nationally and internationally as a pro-athlete, writer, speaker, collegiate coach, hitting instructor and Certified Intrinsic Coach®. As a Pro Speaker for Sports World, Inc. Butler travels the country speaking to more than 40,000 people annually. She is the author of *Prep Steps: 31 day guide to success for female Student-Athletes* and the developer of the Fi Hitting System™. Charity is a recognized expert in confidence training and presents at various conferences and universities. Butler is also the founder of Exceed Sports, LLC (www.exceed-sports.com) and the *I Heart Fastpitch* campaign (www.iheartfastpitch.com). To learn more or schedule Confidence Coaching sessions for an athlete email admin@exceed-sports.com. Follow Charity Twitter/Instagram: @CharityButler

Charlie Dobbins

"A Completely Different Ball Game"

First of all, I would like to thank Gary and Fastpitch.TV for allowing me to participate and write a chapter in "The Fastpitch Book". He has assembled a talented group of coaches, whose passion for the games and the athletes they coach are truly inspirational. Our sport needs leaders with this type of vision, as we grow internationally and compete for the best female athletes as they chose between the other major female sports (volleyball, basketball, lacrosse, soccer).

I have decided to comment about the **role of athletics in higher education, the recruitment process, and the mental aspect of playing college softball**. These are issues and factors that change daily in our busy world, and can be a challenge to all potential collegiate student athletes as well as their families.

The role of athletics in higher education should be to provide a support system that will promote academic success, a positive athletic experience, and overall personal growth for the student athlete. I believe participation in athletics should be a positive experience in which the physical welfare of the student-athlete is paramount. The primary emphasis of the athletic program should be placed on enhancing the personal development of the student-athlete. I also recognize that winning is a legitimate objective, when achieved in an ethical manner.

Coaches should be considered educators and coaching is a specialized form of teaching. Their curriculums should stress the values of training, strategy, teamwork, vigorous competition, and winning and losing, which are all part of a sound educational experience. In addition, establish policies for sportsmanship and ethical conduct consistent with the educational goals of the institution. The goals of the intercollegiate athletic program should be sufficient to the challenge the abilities of the coaching staff, to merit the interest and support of the student body and school staff, and to command the respect of the communities in which we are located.

Athletics should be one part of the total educational experience at the college. Athletes are students and students are athletes. The athletic program exists only because the academic program exists, supporting it and not detracting from it. Participation on an athletic team is a privilege, which should be earned daily by the student athlete.

Athletics has a very <u>important place</u> in the educational process. We as coaches cannot make the mistake with our athletes of emphasizing that participating on an athletic team is the only place where success can be achieved. We need to create a balanced approach, which rewards success in the classroom as while maintaining excellence on the playing field. The push to focus entirely on their particular sport at the expense of all other activities, gives our athletes an unhealthy emphasis on where to place commitment and hard work, when in reality we want our athletes to learn that such effort is required and the proper approach to everything in life. These are teaching points that we as coaches need to emphasize daily as they translate to success in all aspects of our athlete's lives.

Don't make your signing day the greatest day of your career...

The emphasis on getting the coveted "college scholarship" should not overshadow the main reason for attending college: to create a path of success through the education for the rest of your life while giving you a chance to continue your athletic career for another 4 years. Being a star athlete is a dream that everyone who has ever played a competitive sport strives for. The cold hard reality is that there are a lot of "star athletes", all with the same dreams.

The NCAA regulates the number of scholarships that Division I and Division II are allowed to award. The distribution of these monies changes yearly as kids graduate and new players cycle into a program. The number for Division I scholarships is around 12 and Division II is around 7. Most teams carry 24-28 players. This is also assuming that the programs are fully funded, which means their university supports them with full scholarship dollars. Athletic conferences can also limit the amount of scholarship dollars per sport in an effort to maintain competitive balance. Division III does not award any monies based on athletic potential. All of their monies are merit and need based.

Schools are not limited in the amount of financial aid they can grant to individuals. The monies are academic performance based and do not discriminate between athletes and non-athletes. 98% of the students (athletes and non-athletes) receive financial aid while attending college. Other monies can be awarded after the parents have completed the FAFSA forms and the family EFC (estimated family contribution) is generated. This is where any need-based monies are awarded (i.e. Pell, Stafford, etc.), based on a family's income.

Athletic scholarships are limited on availability and renewable every year. Merit based awards are for 4 years and are renewed every year as long as the student meets the minimum gpa determined by the school.

If you eliminate all schools without athletic scholarships, you eliminate nearly half of your options for college softball. Parents and players should ask themselves, "Which is more important? My ego or my wallet?" An education is one of the greatest gifts you can give or receive. If someone offers you any way to pay for part of your education, take the money and run! Start the process early when looking at schools; ask hard questions to the coaches involved. Understand the requirements of attendance and eligibility.

One last point: Division I is only an athletic level, not a measure of the quality of academic programs. Secondly, are you really good enough to play Division I sports, or will you be stuck on a bench or practice squad when you could be playing at another school at the Division II or Division III level? Take time to honestly assess your talent against the level of play on the field.

College Recruiting Myths, Truths and Secrets…the stuff they don't tell you…

If you really want to play softball in college, make sure you and your parents don't waste one minute sitting around talking about how great a player you are; don't compare yourself to other athletes and assume just because they got a scholarship, you're bound to be offered one. Finding a job might be the most important thing in your life once you graduate college, so make your college and team search a practice run. Develop a plan of action; investigate all opportunities and listen to all suggestions; be assertive and willing to work hard; and, most importantly, never give up. Assuming that you are academically and athletically on track to compete in college, I guarantee you will find a team to play for if you meet these three criteria:

1). You, the athlete, want to play softball in college because you love the game and want more than anything else to continue competing.

You must want to play for yourself, not for mom and/or dad, your coaches, or because your friends are doing it.

2). You and your family are willing to do whatever it takes to find a team, including putting lots of work into your college search if necessary.

3). You and your family are willing to look at many different options, i.e., you should consider all types of softball teams and find the one that offers you the chance to make a contribution, while at the same time allowing you to provide the path to get the education you need.

A checklist of what to do, what not to do and "can they do that?"
This is kind of like the old Clint Eastwood movie, The Good, the Bad and the Ugly.

The Good (The truths)

i. You are allowed to make the first contact with programs you are interested in.
ii. Attending camps and showcase events enhance your opportunity of being seen.
iii. Assistant coaches are a great resource and in many instances have responsibility for recruiting.
iv. Coaches do check on your social media habits.
v. College athletic experience creates leadership, pride and loyalty.
vi. Programs need depth, not superstars.
vii. The average D1 softball scholarship in 2014 was $14,713.00 and DII 2014 was $7018.00
viii. Participating in college athletics creates lifelong friendships and contacts.

The Bad (The myths)

i. I can walk on at the school of my choice and eventually get playing time

ii. College coaches can help me get in if I am not academically strong.

iii. If you receive a letter from a coach, you are getting recruited.

iv. My High School / Travel ball coach handles all my recruiting stuff.

v. Recruiting starts senior year.

vi. If I'm a good player, the offers will come.

vii. It's Div. I or it is not worth my time.

viii. Not all student-athletes eligible for graduation from their high school are eligible by NCAA standards

The Ugly (The secrets)

i. Forget about playing Div. I and being a Pre-Med, Education or any other time-intensive major.

ii. Your scholarship could disappear based on your performance. They are 1-year awards.

iii. Your competition is nationwide and international.

iv. You're going to work like a dog: 20 hour practice limit, plus "voluntary" conditioning and weights and then there is class and study hall.

v. Softball is an equivalency sport, which means it can award partial scholarships.

The mental aspect of playing college softball starts with the **coach** and must be owned by the **player.**

"Why do you want to play?"

"What drives you to play?"

Most players really have fun playing this game. Some can't think of playing anything else. All want to continue playing in college. You all have different reasons for playing, but if you are going to spend all this time at practices and games, you might as well develop an attitude to get better. This is where your coach cannot help you. This is where your parents cannot help you. This is where your teammates cannot help you.

Your dedication comes from within. You cannot become the best you can be if you find excuses not to improve. You cannot improve if you find excuses not to practice at home. You cannot improve if you do not or cannot honestly evaluate your mistakes, take responsibility for your own deficiencies, and work to improve them.

Team Breakdowns, the unexpected beats you every time!!!

This is a simple concept that most coaches fail to realize. Time should be set aside during practice for the mental approach to the game. Make it interesting enough so they pay attention and retain what it is you are telling them. To think that strategy is instinctive can lead to disaster and disappointment.

First step is for you to make sure they learn and understand the different points of interest and strategy that your are emphasizing. Demand that your players spend some of their own time working on being a better player.

Give this a try and instead of moaning: "I thought she knew that!" you can now say: "She should have known that".

What's the difference? How can you be upset with someone who doesn't know what to do if they have never been taught it? If you have spent the time to teach and they didn't feel the importance to learn what it is you taught, be upset!!

Don't take the "I didn't understand what you meant" line. Did they ask questions when you discussed it? If not, then there should be some kind of disciplinary action taken to show to everyone how important these strategy talks and drills are.

The key to success is to make it interesting enough for them to learn BEFORE they are used as an example of what not to do next time the team talks about. It will win you games!!!!

Five things a Coach should do every game:

- Stress to your players that we play ourselves every game, and that we are our toughest opponents.
- Make everyone responsible and share the ownership of the results.
- Acknowledge all of their contributions, no matter how large or small.
- Treat everyone as a member of the team
- Share the glory!!!!!!!!

About Charlie Dobbins

Charlie Dobbins is the original orchestrator of the William Peace University softball program. He built the program at WPU from the ground up, establishing the Pacers as a consistent contender in the USA South Athletic Conference. In 15 seasons under Dobbins, WPU has won an average of more than 20 games per year while producing 44 USA

South All Conference and 10 NFCA All Region selections, as well as 119 Academic All Conference and 49 Academic All American members. Coach Dobbins achieved a coaching milestone in 2014 with his 300th career win.

In addition to coaching at WPU, Dobbins has served on several committees including the NFCA/USA Today Division III Top 25 Committee, the NFCA Division III All-America and Coaching Staff of the Year Committee. Coach Dobbins currently serves as the Atlantic Region Representative to the NCAA Division III National Softball Committee. His term runs through 2017.

An accomplished softball player in his own right, Dobbins toured with the World famous *King and His Court* and *King of Diamonds* fastpitch teams and helped retire the "Court" in 2011, ending a 65-year run of touring that covered over 4 million miles, 14,000 games, and over 100 countries. As their "catcher" the last 10 years, he caught the last pitch in the last game ever played. Dobbins' playing experience gives him a unique perspective and helps him communicate effectively with his players. He uses a hands-on approach with his team, focusing on goal-setting and player development.

Darrick Brown

"Work + Love + Faith = Success"

Three things sit fresh in my mind after my current season coaching that equal success: work, love, and faith! With these three things present, anything is possible.

Work

Jim Harbaugh recently tweeted: Attacking the day with enthusiasm unknown to mankind.

Work starts with enthusiasm. Check your life problems at the door and attack the task your coaches put in front of you with insane enthusiasm. Think about it: enthusiasm is defined as intense and eager enjoyment. If every athlete brings that to work then we have an amazing hard working practice. Daily, weekly, monthly, and seasonal goals will be crushed!

In Philippians 2:14-15 it says do all things without grumbling or questioning, that you may be blameless and innocent, children of God without blemish in the midst of a crooked and twisted generation, among whom you shine as lights in the world.

Don't be a cancer to your team, be the light of your team! As the verse says, do all things without grumbling or questioning. You are not entitled, so do what you're told. Nobody wants spoiled athletes who constantly question everything the team is doing. Get on board and the ride will be worth every second!

"Don't be afraid of hard work." – Marian Wright Edelman

I love reading about the Navy SEALs because they may have the best work ethic, team mentality, and brotherhood of any team on the planet. As one of the toughest programs for special operations in the world, the regular dropout rate is about 80 percent. Pretty sure most of us would sit in the 80% dropout rate if we attempted it. However, their strong work ethic and discipline can be carried over onto the softball field by mastering some of their key work ethical practices and strengths as listed.

- Full efforts into training programs
- Work effectively as a team
- Work effectively autonomously
- Remain calm during stressful situations
- Focus your full attention to the task at hand
- Keep confidential work information confidential
- Be the best of the best – always!

Following the above and pushing your body to do real work will get you results beyond your wildest imagination. God has given us this amazing vessel called the human body that can do way beyond what most of us do on a daily basis. In the movie Lone Survivor, the team takes multiple jumps down a mountain to flee from the enemy. During the firefight, multiple bone fractures, cuts, bruises, and bullet wounds occurred but the team kept going. The SEALs are trained to keep going, finish the mission, and to do things with such precision that casualties rarely occur. It all begins with the work they put in from day one! Push past your limits!

Love

"Teamwork is what the Green Bay Packers were all about. They didn't do it for individual glory. They did it because they loved one another." - Vince Lombardi

Love needs to be present, especially love for your teammates! Love creates a family atmosphere and sisterhood. When you have that you have something special. Players will push each other and get the best out of each other. They will go out of their way to support each other on and off the field. They will be hardcore cheerleaders for their teammates. Players in a sisterhood atmosphere are selfless and will do anything to make the TEAM better.

Be kind and compassionate to one another, forgiving each other, just as in Christ God forgave you. –Ephesians 4:32

There will always be drama moments! We aren't dealing with perfect human beings. You will be annoyed, frustrated, mad, or sick to your stomach over a teammate's decision or behavior. Love and forgiveness can make that go away when you truly care about and love your teammates.

If I have the gift of prophecy and can fathom all mysteries and all knowledge, and if I have a faith that can move mountains, but have not love, I am nothing. – 1 Corinthians 13:2

Without the love of the game you have nothing. I see a lot of really talented players who are playing on the best teams and training with the top instructors, but they don't love the game. Many play for other reasons, like playing to make their parents happy. We do player surveys where I coach so I can gather information and determine the mindset of our players. One of the big questions in my eyes is asking why they play the game. I ask them to be specific and answer with some body to their answer. I get a big range of answers but my hope is that they simply love the game. When you love something you will be motivated to work hard to make it the best experience possible.

You can love a guy up and [still] create an environment that's conducive to winning. – Michael Robinson when talking about Seattle Seahawks Coach Pete Carroll

We can't force or mandate love, but we can create an environment where love flourishes on its own. The coaches and team leaders from day one can set the foundation for this and throughout the season must maintain it. My advice to the athlete: never take what a coach says personally because they are simply trying to get the best out of you. If your coach is doing it for the right reason he loves you! My advice to the coach: When you get personal, it's time to find another profession. Love your kids, all of them! Love even the rotten apples because they need your love and support the most.

Faith

Growing up with a Dad and seven uncles who all played men's fastpitch, I learned quickly what intense competition meant. Fastpitch was like a secondary religion in my family and it consumed a great deal of the summer days of my childhood. My Dad and uncles were like major leaguers to me. I watched very closely and that fire and competitiveness they played with was quickly embedded in me. That fire carried over into my coaching; especially as a young coach, I hated to lose. I remember my first coaching job and we were 34-2. Man those 2 losses were devastating to me! The girls didn't understand why they had to run during a near perfect season but I just wanted them to hate losing as much as I did. It continued for years and years at every level and even when I coached the Chicago Bandits to the 2011 National Pro Fastpitch Championship. I was told regular season didn't matter many times because it just determined the seeding for the end. I couldn't in my competitive mind accept that and it ate at me and I really stressed to the point where I wasn't enjoying what should've been the best coaching job of my life. Don't get me wrong, it was a great summer and a big moment in my coaching career, but I wish I had the maturity in my faith like I have today.

For God so loved the world that he gave his one and only Son, that whoever believes in him shall not perish but have eternal life. –John 3:16

Fast-forward to now and a more mature me. I'm not going to sit here and say that I don't hate losing still, but I have this amazing peacefulness in me that only God can give me. I react differently, see differently, hear differently, speak differently, and think differently knowing that God is with me every step of the way. Believing in the verse above just puts life into a different perspective for me. The father loves us so much that he gave his son so we could have eternal life. No loss in a softball game can take that away from me.

"Devote yourselves to prayer, being watchful and thankful." - Colossians 4:2

At my current job at Kellogg CC, we pray before every game. My favorite pictures of this season are of the team huddling and praying. One of my players posted on one of these pictures of us praying and commented: A team that prays together stays together. I believe in that comment 100%. We won the conference championship, state championship, and broke win and home run records this season, so there are a lot of great memories but the time in that huddle, thanking the Father together, is priceless and bigger than any win. We recently had our end of the year party and we had the team and several family members there. The team sat at a long table together and I was off sitting in a chair by one of the Dads. I looked at the team table and they were holding hands and praying in front of everybody. It took a lot for me to hold back from bawling my eyes out! You can take all of my wins away and give me that moment right there. It put an exclamation point on the end of the season.

About Darrick Brown

Coach Brown brings 23 years of coaching experience to the table. He is also a 26-year veteran of men's fastpitch and a 2011 member of the King and His Court. In his career at the JUCO level, he averaged more than 30 wins per season and coached teams to two consecutive MCCAA West titles during his three-year stint with Glen Oaks Community College (2005) and Kalamazoo Valley Community College (2006). In 2006, KVCC led the country in home runs with 76 in a season and the team finished ranked seventh in the country. In 2011, Coach Brown was head coach of the Chicago Bandits, winning the National Pro Fastpitch Championship series. Brown was the pitching coach at Davenport University in 2012 and 2013, during which time DU won a WHAC regular season title (2012) and a WHAC tournament title (2013).

Coach Brown also runs his own softball and baseball training facility called Brown's Fastpitch, which is located in Kalamazoo. Brown's Fastpitch houses multiple softball and baseball travel teams that compete nationally.

Joni Frei

"Program Design and Implementation; Developing the Grassroots"

Over the years people have asked if I have ever written a book. The truth is, I don't know that I have enough useful information upstairs to necessitate writing an entire book; however, I do believe that the information in this chapter can be an asset to the club or organization interested in implementing a softball or baseball program for children 8 years and younger. The beauty in this system is that you do not need to have an extensive background in softball or baseball to coach. In fact, it's almost better that you don't because you will not have the paradigms to limit you. This program focuses primarily on fundamental skill development and acquisition while ensuring a fun and exciting atmosphere with maximum activity. It is through my experiences as a teacher, college coach, gold level travel ball coach, 12U coach, 10U coach, program facilitator and now 6U coach that I have gained this knowledge. Excellence is in the details, and it is the **details and organization** of this program that makes it work.

According to the Coaching Association of Canada, some key growth and development concepts for this age range include: self-esteem and the perception of success are strongly linked; observing, quickly followed by doing is the best method for learning; the attention span lasts only a few minutes; the dominant side is established; imagination or imitation contribute to the enjoyment of activities; games should have few rules; modified equipment should be used; a generous dose of praise for efforts is needed; techniques and analogies that stimulate imagination should be used; child is egocentric and individualistic. It is important to avoid lengthy explanations as well as comparisons with other children. These concepts are recognized in this program.

Below you will see two sample practices of a program that lasts 3 months in which the kids meet twice a week. Each session lasts an hour and a half and is divided into 5 main parts which include: **warm up, fundamental skill development, game play, teamwork and review**. A head coach or facilitator is needed with a minimum of 8 parent-coaches. The ideal ratio is a 4:1 kids to coach. This program can be run on 1 full sized softball field further divided into 4 smaller fields. Field 1 is the main field in which the warm up activities are done, field 2 is in right field, field 3 is in centre field and field 4 is in left field. Each field has a set of bases for game play which takes place after skill development.

Equipment requirements are dependent upon the abilities and number of children in the program and can include: bow nets/screens, tees, rubber balls/blast balls, tennis balls, tennis racquets, bean bags, helmets, blast ball bases/regular bases, home plates, hoola-hoops, agility ladders, beach balls, teddy bears, oven mitts, playground balls, foam blast ball bats/plastic bats, cones, numbered pylons.

Warm-up consists of agility and coordination exercises through four agility ladders that are placed between the (blast ball) bases on the base-lines of the main field. For example there is a ladder between home and 1st, 1st and 2nd etc. The kids will gather themselves on the base-paths and collectively go through the ladders, jogging when not going through a ladder and stepping on each base as they pass.

Fundamental skill development is achieved primarily at stations. Kids learn and practice two new skills per day - 4 skills per week (based on two practices a week). Skills will be revisited throughout the program and cues will build on each other. The activities and drills will progress. There are progressions and regressions to skill development. Modified equipment will encourage skill development, such as using oven mitts instead of gloves.

Game play is a modified game in which there should be no more than 6 players on a team. The field will be divided into 4 smaller fields. Games will start with players hitting off a tee until they are ready to transition into front toss (by the coach or spring loaded pitching machine). Players will start the season going one base at a time after hitting the ball and transition into advancing multiple bases when they are ready. The last batter will run all of the bases and all base runners will run home. Use sponge bats and either tennis balls or blast balls when playing. Initially, the only play that needs to be made by the defense is a throw to first base. The entire team will bat and then transition into offense and defense respectively. Players will rotate positions each inning so no player plays the same position twice in a game. Have the offensive team "sit down" in a line when waiting to hit.

Teamwork is demonstrated during the base-race after the game. One team lines up at home plate the other team lines up at 2nd base (on their respective fields). The parent-coach yells "go" and one person from each team runs around all of the bases and returns to where they started passing the ball to the next player to run with.

Review happens after the base races when everyone gathers around the pitching circle on the main field. It is used to check for understanding and guide future practice plans. Head coach/facilitator will ask questions pertaining to cues that were taught that day and demonstrate a movement asking them what animal is associated with that skill.

Safety concerns to be cognizant of: kids swinging bats not paying attention to who is around; balls being thrown when the partner is not ready; a line of kids standing on the backside of the person hitting the ball; throwing of the bat; partners of extreme skill differences. Please teach "safety rules" early and often.

Organizational tips: Head coach/facilitator will email to parent-coaches the weekly practice plans Sunday night. Playing fields need to be set up ahead of time so kids can transition from stations to their game immediately without needing much set up time. When rotating stations the parent-coach should go to the station they are receiving players from to "pick up" their kid (this will help keep kids from getting lost ☺). Parent-coaches should know what color team they are starting with that day (it will be the same every other practice). Kids rotate stations while parent-coaches stay at their own station. Each team has a different color jersey/shirt and number assignment. An example is: "Team Black" is associated with number 1; "Team Red" is associated with number 2 and so on. **The coach that the team started with on the first day of the program is their coach for games throughout the season.**

TIME LINE:
Mondays & Wednesdays   6:00pm to 7:30pm

    5:30pm Head coach/facilitator arrives and marks off field with pylons so parent-coaches know where to set up their station

    5:35pm Parent-coaches arrive to set up their station

    5:55pm Kids arrive

    6:00pm to 6:10pm Kids perform coordination & agility drills around the bases (Head Coach)

    6:10pm Group cheer "softball rocks!" and players go to their coaches for the first station

    6:15pm to 6:30pm Station 1 (Parent-Coaches)

    6:30pm to 6:35pm Transition to next station (Parent-Coaches "pick up" players)

    6:35pm to 6:50pm Station 2 (Parent-Coaches)

    6:50pm to 6:55pm Parent-coach transition to one of the four different fields

6:55pm to 7:15pm Modified games

7:15pm to 7:25pm Base-race at each field (Parent-Coaches)

7:25-7:30pm Review and check for understanding (Head Coach/ Facilitator)

Sample Practice Plan Rotation 1 & 2

Rotation 1		Team	Skills	Cues
Coach 1	Station 1	Black	Overhand Throw	Cue "names"
Coach 2	Station 2	Yellow	Catching Above & Below	Cue "names"
Coach 3	Station 3	Light Blue	Fielding Ball front & lateral	Cue "names"
Coach 4	Station 4	Orange	Hitting Off Tee	Cue "names"
Coach 5	Station 5	Navy Blue	Overhand Throw	Cue "names"
Coach 6	Station 6	Green	Catching Above & Below	Cue "names"
Coach 7	Station 7	Red	Fielding Ball front & lateral	Cue "names"
Coach 8	Station 8	Maroon	Hitting Off Tee	Cue "names"
Rotation 2		**Team**	**Skills**	**Cues**
Coach 1	Station 1	Orange	Overhand Throw	Cue "names"
Coach 2	Station 2	Black	Catching Above & Below	Cue "names"
Coach 3	Station 3	Yellow	Fielding Ball front & lateral	Cue "names"
Coach 4	Station 4	Light Blue	Hitting Off Tee	Cue "names"
Coach 5	Station 5	Maroon	Overhand Throw	Cue "names"
Coach 6	Station 6	Navy Blue	Catching Above & Below	Cue "names"
Coach 7	Station 7	Green	Fielding Ball front & lateral	Cue "names"
Coach 8	Station 8	Red	Hitting Off Tee	Cue "names"

Rotations 1 & 2 Explained

Stations 1 & 4

Equipment: Cones, Hula Hoop, Mixed Balls
Location Station 1: 3rd Base Fence
Location Station 5: 1st Base Fence
Drill: Throwing into hoola hoop, behind cones
(gradually increase distance)

Skill: Throwing Overhand
(Contralateral & Rotation)
Cues: "eagle wings" (elbows stay high) &
"finish belly-button to target" (hips &
shoulders rotate)

Stations 2 & 5

Equipment: Oven Mitts, Mixed Balls
Location: Left field foul line (short)
Location: Right field foul line (short)
Drill: Catching balls tossed from coach
(gradually increase distance)

Skill: Catching Above The Waist
Cues: "Elk Antlers"
(thumbs together, eyes looking over fingers above
the head)

Skill: Catching Below Waist
Cues: "Squid Fingers" (pinky fingers together)

Stations 3 & 7

Equipment: Cones, Hula Hoop, Mixed Balls
Location Station 3: Shortstop Grass
Location Station 7: Second Base Grass
Drill: Fielding ground balls rolled in front or to the side of a player

Skill: Fielding a ball hit straight towards the player
Cues: "alligator"

Skill: Fielding a ball hit laterally
Cues: "monkey shuffle"

Stations 4 & 8

Equipment: Bow Net, Mixed Balls, Tees
Location Station 4: Left field foul line (deep)
Location Station 8: Right field foul line (deep)
Drill: Hitting off tees into Bow Nets

Skill: Hitting A Ball Off Of A Tee:
Cues: "mike & ike"
(start with hands at back shoulder, "mike" & finish with hands on front shoulder "ike")

Field Dimensions & Rotation Explanation

You may have noticed that stations 5-8 are the same skills and cues as 1-4. If you look back to the sample practice plans you will see the location of each station. Stations 1-4 are on the left side of the diamond and stations 5-8 are on the right side of the diamond. This means that teams on the left side of the field rotate amongst themselves. For example: Station 1 team rotates to station 2, station 2 team rotates to station 3, station 3 team rotates to station 4 and station 4 team rotates to station 1. The same is true for the right side of the field. Station 5 team rotates to station 6, station 6 team rotates to station 7, station 7 team rotates to station 8 and station 8 team rotates to station 5. For games the regulation-sized field is divided into 4 smaller fields. Remember 2 skills are covered per practice, 4 skills per week. This means that after one week the teams have been to all four stations. Each week a new set of practice plans is given to the parent-coaches. Next week's practice plan may involve more hitting stations and a base-running station for example.

Sample Practice Plan Rotation 3 & 4

Rotation 3			Team	Skills	Cues
Coach 1	Station 1		Orange	Overhand Throw	Cue "names"
Coach 2	Station 2		Light Blue	Catching Above & Below	Cue "names"
Coach 3	Station 3		Black	Fielding Ball front & lateral	Cue "names"
Coach 4	Station 4		Yellow	Hitting Off Tee	Cue "names"
Coach 5	Station 5		Red	Overhand Throw	Cue "names"
Coach 6	Station 6		Maroon	Catching Above & Below	Cue "names"
Coach 7	Station 7		Navy Blue	Fielding Ball front & lateral	Cue "names"
Coach 8	Station 8		Green	Hitting Off Tee	Cue "names"
Rotation 4			Team	Skills	Cues
Coach 1	Station 1		Yellow	Overhand Throw	Cue "names"
Coach 2	Station 2		Orange	Catching Above & Below	Cue "names"
Coach 3	Station 3		Light Blue	Fielding Ball front & lateral	Cue "names"
Coach 4	Station 4		Black	Hitting Off Tee	Cue "names"
Coach 5	Station 5		Green	Overhand Throw	Cue "names"
Coach 6	Station 6		Red	Catching Above & Below	Cue "names"
Coach 7	Station 7		Maroon	Fielding Ball front & lateral	Cue "names"
Coach 8	Station 8		Navy Blue	Hitting Off Tee	Cue "names"

Rotations 3 & 4 Explained

You'll notice that the only differences between practice plan 1 and practice plan 2 are the team at the station. For example practice 1 "Team Black" started at station 1 and finished at station 2, so on practice 2 they will start at station 3 and finish at station 4. The benefit to this is once you have a set template the only things that need to change from week to week are the skills and cues. It's that easy!

Game Schedule

Field 1 (main field)	**Team 1: Black VS Team 2: Yellow**
Field 2 (right field)	**Team 3: Orange VS Team 4: Light Blue**
Field 3 (center field)	**Team 5: Navy Blue VS Team 6: Green**
Field 4 (left field)	**Team 7: Red VS Team 8: Maroon**

About Joni Frei

Joni Frei graduated with a degree in Kinesiology and a minor in Health Sciences with Teacher Certification from Georgia College & State University. There she helped lead her team to a 2nd place finish at the NCAA Division II National Tournament. Joni broke a number of school records at Georgia College & State University including home runs, walks, RBI's and runs scored. She was the recipient of many prestigious academic and athletic awards including NCAA National Tournament Team, All Conference Player Awards, University Athlete of the Year, and Department of Health Sciences Student of The Year.

After graduating, Joni moved to Europe to play in Holland. Upon the end of her competitive playing career, she returned to the United States to pursue a career in coaching as an assistant with Kennesaw State University under Hall Of Fame Coach, Scott Whitlock. At Kennesaw State University, Joni earned a Master's degree in Political Science with a concentration in Public Administration. Joni has coached at all levels of softball including serving as the head coach of the Austrian National Team, Assistant Coach for Division I Kennesaw State University, Assistant Coach for Division I Mercer University, Assistant Coach for NAIA Reinhardt College and Assistant Coach for Georgia Military College. Currently, Joni is owner of Beyond The White Lines Softball Academy, Technical Director for South Surrey Minor Softball Association, Head Coach of The Canada Futures College Exposure Team, Softball B.C. Learning Facilitator, and Director of Coaching for Softball BC.

If you have any questions or if you would like a complete program that includes even more specific details with 16 practice plans free of charge. Contact: jonifrei@yahoo.com

Kaci Clark Zerbe

"The Popular Myth that Could Keep You From Pitching in College"

Many of you have wondered why college coaches choose to recruit some pitchers and not others. A coach may watch you throw a no hitter and win by 10 runs, but pass you by to recruit the pitcher from the other team. What is that all about?!

Frankly, college coaches worth their salt don't really care if you're winning high school games and beating high school hitters. You're not coming to their school to pitch against high school hitters. Therefore, they are looking for the tools they know it takes to beat hitters at their level of the game.

Typically, there are four physical tools they're looking for -- velocity, command, spin, and a GREAT change up. There are a few mental tricks that will help you become an All-American once you get recruited, but that's not our current subject, so I'll just say this: Be aware of your body language and presence! You don't turn on the TV and see pitchers in the Women's College World Series complaining about balls and strikes, pouting over blown plays, and arguing with their coaches or teammates for all to see. Players like that often derail a team's success. You can have great physical tools and almost every college coach in the country will mark you off their recruiting list for these offenses.

With that said, let's address one of the most common myths that gets repeated so often that it stops many from getting recruited and leaves pitchers all over the country baffled about what they're doing wrong in the recruiting process. This myth is that "speed doesn't matter, it's all about spin and location". I even heard a commentator (who threw 70+ mph by the way) repeat this statement during the Women's College World Series!

When it comes to recruiting, speed is like the secret password that either gets you in the club or keeps you out. The next time someone tells you that speed doesn't matter, ask yourself when you last saw a pitcher in the WCWS throwing 54 miles an hour? I can think of two pitchers who made multiple appearances in the WCWS throwing less than 60 mph. But both of them were throwing higher than 60 when they were recruited and sustained injuries during their college careers that reduced their speed. So don't misunderstand, you can succeed at the college level throwing less than 60, it's getting recruited that can be difficult. In my experience, people who believe this myth and repeat it have one of three major reasons for believing it.

1. <u>They believe that speed cannot be taught.</u> <u>You either have it or you don't, so you might as well just work on spin and location.</u>

The speed of your pitch is a combination of how strong you are plus how fast you move. That's why among the elite levels of power pitchers (68mph and up), you will see different types of deliveries and different body types. Some mistakenly believe that you have to be tall or "big" to throw hard. I, Lisa Fernandez, Taryne Mowatt, Amanda Scarborough, Gina Oaks, Lisa Longaker, and countless others who were between 5'3" and 5'6" and threw anywhere from 65-73 would love to respectfully disagree (or laugh at them if given the chance). We were not giants, but we were strong and moved fast and those two things equal velocity. That's also why not every 6'2" pitcher throws 70. It takes an exceptional amount of strength to move a frame that size quickly enough to generate those kinds of numbers. But one cannot argue that a larger frame can have the potential for more strength than a smaller frame.

As far as delivery keys to velocity, there are no magic fixes. You can't just change the way your foot turns and go from 55 to 65. You have to be able to move towards the catcher as fast as you can, in the strongest position possible without getting in your own way. For example, if your hips are wider than your shoulders, and your pitching arm consistently makes contact with your hip before you release the ball, your arm will be slowing as you release as opposed to accelerating or at least maintaining speed. This results in a slower pitch. If all of your weight is consistently out on your front foot early in your delivery, your body's innate sense of balance will pull you back to upright before you release as opposed to letting you continue forward motion (in a strong position) toward the catcher, typically resulting in a slower pitch. There are those who are strong enough and move fast enough to overcome these delivery issues, but they are few and far between.

Beyond that, people will always argue about mechanics, but as long as you can move as fast as possible, in a strong position toward the catcher, your velocity will have the opportunity to max out.

2. <u>They believe that, as long as you practice enough, you will throw hard enough</u>.

I'm sure that you've heard by now that the definition of insanity is doing the same thing over and over again and expecting different results. That is precisely what you are doing if you expect daily, repetitive practice to somehow make you move faster. Yet, so many still advise you to wear your body out with a prescription of 150-200 pitches a day to increase speed. There are only two times in a pitcher's life when she can "accidentally" gain velocity just by repeating her movements. 1. When she is first learning to pitch and repeating the series of movements allows her to merge those movements into one fluid motion. and 2. After major growth spurts when the pitcher becomes bigger and stronger without much concerted effort.

Beyond that, a pitcher must challenge herself in ways that make her stronger and/or faster. Most of my favorite strength and speed work (especially for younger pitchers) does not involve weights. You can increase strength with pitching drills like long toss (with correct delivery) or simply throwing fastballs from 46ft at the end of your pitching workouts. You can increase speed with an easy 30, 20, 10 drill. Have someone time you while you throw as many fastballs as possible in 30 seconds. You can do this with or without a catcher, just be sure to back up enough between each pitch to be able to start from approximately the same area. Catchers won't play this game with you if you continue to advance on them every pitch for 30 seconds while throwing as hard as you can. After resting for 150 seconds (5 seconds for every 1 second you were in motion), try 20 seconds. After 20 seconds, rest for 100 seconds, Then try 3 sets of 10 seconds with 50 seconds of rest in between each set. YOU MUST INCREASE YOUR NUMBERS OVER TIME IN ORDER TO INCREASE SPEED!! If you're not sure why, refer back to the first part of this section containing the definition of insanity.

I grew up in a state that had its fair share of cold weather, so pitching wasn't always an option. Frankly, your body needs a break from pitching for a little while every year. My favorite ways to increase strength and speed without weights or pitching are plyometrics, agilities, and sprint work. If you are working for speed, avoid long, slow running. Pitching is not slow, nor should your workout be! Distance running is not bad exercise, but it will not increase your speed or your pitching stamina.

3. <u>Perhaps they haven't spent much time successfully helping pitchers get recruited at the top levels of our sport</u>.

If you're wondering why speed matters so much, bear in mind that the purpose of spin and location is to fool batters about the final location of the pitch as it crosses the plate. If they have all day to figure out where it's going, it's tough to fool a good hitter.

Many people see "spin pitchers" like Cat Osterman and Blair Luna and cling to the "speed doesn't matter" myth because they are not known to be "power pitchers". These two spin pitchers are still easily topping 60 mph. In 20 years of helping pitchers get recruited, here is what I find to be the benchmark of the moment. A number with a 6 in front is typically required just to pique the interest of a top school. A number less than 60 will typically not result in much response at all. A 60-61 usually receives a, "she sounds great, now excuse me while I go recruit the ones throwing 65 and I'll come back to her if everyone else falls through". Once we get to 62-63, THEN they'll ask how well she spins and locates. At 64-65, they'll be willing to come see how well she spins and locates. At 66 plus, they'll invite you to come see them, especially if you possess a shadow of the other three physical weapons I mentioned above.

One caveat: someone with "experience" guessing how hard you throw "because they've seen 65 and know what it looks like" WILL NOT CUT IT!!! I cannot count the number of disillusioned pitchers I've worked with who relied on someone's eye only to get on a radar gun as a high school junior and find out that their "that's definitely more than 60" turned out to be 56-57. You must get on a real radar gun (preferably the same one) on a regular basis (ideally once a month). Pocket radars are fairly inexpensive, fairly accurate, and available online. Know where you stand and work hard at it. 60+ miles per hour is no accident for most pitchers, it takes hard, consistent WORK!! It is possible!

Please remember, no single element of pitching is good enough to stand completely on its own. While speed may get you in the door, speed alone is not pitching and will not get you the full ride every pitcher dreams of. The same can be said of spin, location, and the change up. Think about pitching like you think about math. In order to be able to perform basic math, you must be able to add, subtract, multiply, and divide, You can't be great at addition stink at all the rest and declare yourself a stellar mathematician! If you see college softball in your future, train purposefully for speed in addition to your other tools because, in the world of college recruiting, it really matters.

About Kaci Clark Zerbe

Kaci Clark Zerbe has coached at the NCAA Division 1, NJCAA, high school, and travel ball levels. For the last 15 years, she has been a private pitching instructor and clinician. Her current and past students have represented National Championship teams (as well as teams "in the running") at the NCAA Division 1 and 2, National Pro Fastpitch, ASA, and Premiere Girls' Fastpitch levels. Her students have received Most Outstanding Player at the Division 1 NCAA Women's College World Series, Multiple NCAA and ASA All-American awards (including the first four-time All-American at the University of Florida), and numerous NCAA All-Conference selections as well as Conference Pitcher of the Year accolades. She has also spent time training international pitchers and pitching staffs for Australia, New Zealand, Great Britain, and Germany.

As a player, Kaci began her college career at Georgia State University and completed it at UCLA. She has pitched on six National Championship teams including 1 NCAA, 3 Pro Fastpitch, and back to back ASA Women's Championships with the Stratford Brakettes. She was named an All-American 3 times, a Professional All Star 4 times, the Pro League Pitcher of the Year twice, the Pro League MVP once, and the ASA's Most Outstanding Pitcher. She also competed internationally in Japan for Team Honda, in Australia (awarded the Perth League's Most Outstanding Pitcher), and in New Zealand. She finished her career on the Pro Fastpitch X-Treme tour and finally playing for FCA softball.

Keri Casas

"The Hell Week Pitching Workout"

As our pitchers mature and showcase their ability of consistency and velocity, we want to be careful not to create the same routine for every lesson or workout. Pitchers need to constantly challenge themselves not only for muscle memory, but for endurance, injury prevention, and strength. Varying their workouts allows them to strengthen all muscles necessary for pitching, essentially cross-training the body for optimal performance. Furthermore, the high-intensity and demand of these workouts develops mental toughness and confidence in game situations.

The following drills represent a "Hell Week" workout. These drills are meant to challenge the body and mind through endurance, strength, and mental training. Each day focuses on different aspects of pitching that will all come together to enhance performance. "Hell Week" isn't necessarily meant to be completed every week, but it is recommended at least twice a week to maintain and gain every week.

Day One:

Focus: Leg Drive
Duration: 60 minutes
Warm up: 5 minute jog and stretch. Complete regular pitching warm up until "game ready".

Workout:

The athlete will start with fastballs, keeping her stride as long as possible towards the end of the circle. After throwing 6 pitches, she will do walking lunges towards her catcher and back to the mound and immediately move on to the next pitch. Next, she will throw 6 change ups and complete long jumps to her catcher and back to the mound. She will follow the same pattern with her remaining pitches, cross-training between strength and agility moves. The following are leg drive drills for her to complete between pitches:

- Backwards lunges

- Jump squats

- Side lunges

- Alternating lunge jumps

- Line sprints

- Pile squats (toes pointed out)

- Squat with star jump (athlete squats low and burst up, extending arms and legs out like a star)

- Cross lunges (athlete steps across body and drops down)

The most important factor in this workout is for the athlete to continue leg drive as far as possible on each pitch. Even though she may be tired and her legs feel like jello, this is the best opportunity for her to feel the potential she has in her leg drive. The harder she pushes herself, the easier it will be to drive out when her body is not fatigued.

Cool down: 2 minute jog and leg stretch.

Day Two:

Focus: Endurance
Duration: 60 minutes
Warm Up: 1 mile run and stretch. Attempt for the mile to be between 8:30-9:00 minutes. Ideally, a great mile time would be between 7-7:30 minutes. Complete normal pitching warm up until "game ready".

Workout:

The endurance workout is meant to challenge the body and mind. An athlete's body can always endure more than what their brain tells them. Don't let your athlete quit on this workout!! The more she believes she can push herself and complete this workout without stopping, the more confidence she will have when the game gets tough!

This workout starts with a speed drill. A helper will be at the end of the pitcher's circle with a bucket of balls. The athlete will start at the mound and the helper will toss her a ball. As soon as the ball is tossed the athlete will throw her pitch, the helper will toss her another ball, and she will jog backwards until she is behind the mound. Once they are behind the mound, she will run through the mound and throw the next pitch. She will continue this routine until the bucket is empty. If this is her first time completing a speed drill, I recommend starting with 10 balls, then working towards a whole bucket. She will complete the speed drill 3 times before moving on.

After the speed drill, the athlete will begin her pitching routine. Similar to Day One, your athlete needs to push herself to throw close to 100% as much as possible. The more she can work while she is tired, the easier it gets when her body is at 100%. After each set of pitches, (about 10-12 pitches) your athletes will complete the following set of endurance drills:

- 6- 60ft sprints with jog back

- 20 burpees

- 20 box jumps (you can use bleachers, a bench, etc)

- 4- 60 ft long jumps

- 1 minute plank on all sides each

- 1 minute mountain climbers

If your athlete has more than 6 pitches, start at the first drill until she is done. Naturally, we want to end the endurance workout with a bang; one more speed drill! This time, only use 10 balls and complete the drill 3 times. If your athlete makes it through this workout on the first time, major props!

Cool down: 5 minute jog and stretch

Day Three: Rest and Stretch

She may be tired after her leg and endurance days. Day Three is meant for rest and stretching. Make sure she continues to stay hydrated to prevent muscle cramping and fatigue. It is recommended for your athlete to drink half their body weight in ounces of water every day, (ex. If she weighs 160lbs, she should drink 80 oz of water)! This will keep her hydrated and help increase her performance.

Day Four:

Focus: Mental Strength
Duration: 45-60 minutes (it may take longer)
Warm up: 10 minute jog with stretch. Full pitching warm up.

Workout:

Mental strength day may be my favorite training day out of the whole week. Let's face it; our pitchers can't be "on" every debut. When they don't necessarily have their stuff, mental strength comes into play. As pitchers, we know when we aren't on, and we just have to make it work to get through the game. Mental training is a huge factor in the ability for your athlete to look like she has her stuff on any given day.

This game is called 6 of 6. The athlete will throw their 6 main pitches in this workout. She will start with a fastball on a corner. If she does not hit her spot, she will do an exercise (burpees, pushups, etc). Once she hits her fastball in the right spot, she will move on to throw a fastball, then her second pitch. If she misses her second pitch, she starts over in that sequence, (fastball, change-up). Here is what it looks like:

1: Fastball

2: Fastball, Change-up

3: Fastball, Change-up, Drop

4: Fastball, Change-up, Drop, Curve

5: Fastball, Change-up, Drop, Curve, Screw

6: Fastball, Change-up, Drop, Curve, Screw, Rise

Once she hits 6 of 6, she's done. This may seem like an easy drill, but it creates pressure for your athlete to maintain consistency. We are also creating muscle memory to enhance her ability to hit her spots even with pressure, fatigue, and frustration. This will teach your athlete to work through the frustration and find what her mentality needs to be to complete this drill. Some athletes use anger, some need to be relaxed, and some need to envision the pitch. Every pitcher is different, so whenever she sees success, she needs to tap into what she was doing mentally to maintain consistency.

Cool down: 2 minute jog and stretch.

Day Five:

Focus: Spin
Duration: 30-45 minutes
Warm Up: 10 minute jog with stretch

Workout:

This workout is relatively easy on the body and mainly focuses on wrist snap and body positioning. The athlete will need a baseball or a 10 inch softball. She will use her 3 important fingers, (index, middle, and ring), to complete this drill. She will start about 2 feet from her catcher and complete snaps for all her pitches. Using a small ball forces the athlete to feel how the ball rotates off her fingers and strengthens her grip for snap. After snaps, the athlete will back up to 2 feet in front of the mound and complete "breakdowns" with the small ball.

Breakdowns allow the athlete to walk through her pitch with her wrist snap being her only aggressive move. When she breaks down her pitch, she will be able to see and feel what her body is doing and what she needs to correct. Keeping her wrist snap the hardest part of the pitch allows her to see if she is really snapping or using her arm to finish the pitch. Our focus is to keep the athletes shoulder and bicep relaxed with her forearm, wrist, and fingers doing the work. You will be able to see the difference between good movement and great movement with this drill.

Cool down: 5 minute jog and stretch

Day Six: Rest and Stretch

Day Seven:

Focus: Arm strength
Duration: 30-45 minutes
Warm up: 1 mile run and stretch. Complete game ready warm up

Workout:

Arm strength is a vital aspect of pitching. The most common injury we see in pitching is through the shoulder. We want to prevent injury, fatigue, and weakness as much as possible. To do so, we want to keep both sides of the athlete's body strong. We tend to ignore our glove hand side and build up our throwing arm, which in turn, creates poor muscle develop and leads to injury. Prior to this workout, it is recommended to complete and armband workout for both arms. Tie the band to the fence and work through overhand and underhand rotations, as well as, internal and external rotations. Make sure to complete this on both sides; we want to keep our strength in both arms as equal as possible. After the arm band workout out, your athlete will complete a long toss workout. Long toss is great for overall body strength, but it also teaches the athlete to relax her shoulder and use her forearm and wrist to create power. The ball will travel a greater distance with more speed with a relaxed body and quick snap. The athlete will throw all her pitches from 2nd base or further, about 10 pitches each). A quick note, changes-ups aren't very effective for long toss, so feel free to skip those.

Once she has complete long toss for all pitches, bring her back in to normal pitching distance. From the mound, she will throw 3 of each pitch at 120% percent. When doing so, she needs to make sure she is maintaining pressure in her legs, forearm, and wrist, not her shoulder. When correct, she will see more velocity and movement with far less stress on the body.

Cool Down: 5 minute jog and stretch

Always remember you can make your own "Hell Week", just vary the drills up above and push yourself harder every day. It takes about 4 weeks to fall into a solid routine, so continue to push through "Hell Week" and eventually you won't want to miss these workouts!

About Keri Casas

Keri Casas is the Director of Operations and Lead Instructor for All American Softball, Inc in Sacramento, CA. A former Division 1 student-athlete and graduate of Syracuse University, Keri is a coordinator for All American's College Prep Program, helping athletes achieves collegiate softball scholarships. Keri is also the lead contributor and editor of CoachingaFemaleAthlete.com and co-author of the E-Book, "Bats, Gloves, and Glitter: 7 Must-Know Facts About Female Athletes".

Laura Berg

"The Mindset of an Outfielder"

I remember playing in the 2002 World Championships in Saskatoon, Canada like it happened yesterday. We were playing against Italy and it was a very close game. They were well coached by Judi Garman and we knew we had a fight on our hands. Lisa Fernandez was on the mound and there was a runner on second base with one out. I was playing shallow centerfield to give myself a chance to throw the runner out at home plate if the ball was hit to me. What happened next will prove how important outfielders are. The Italian batter hit a deep fly ball to right center. I took my drop step to my left and ran as fast as I could. I knew I was going to have to dive in order to catch the fly ball. I took approximately 10 running steps, I left my feet and reached for the ball. I caught it and landed on the ground. As soon as I landed, I got up to my feet and threw the ball to third base. The runner on second base tagged up and tried to advance to third. My throw to third was in time and my teammate was able to tag the runner out. That one play shifted the momentum from their dugout to ours. We got out of the inning and ended up beating a very good Italian team in the round robin game.

I'm not telling this story to toot my own horn. I'm telling it so all the youth softball players know how critical outfielders are to the success of the team. When I'm at camps and it's time for the kids to come to my outfield station there is an energy shift. They don't like to play the outfield because they say "it's boring". One of the first things that comes out of my mouth when I talk to young kids is "Outfielders rule!!" I have made it my personal mission to talk about the importance of the outfield to all the kids I work with at camps. It's not boring. There are so many things an outfielder has to do. They have to not only catch the ball when it gets hit to them but they get to make unbelievable diving catches. They get to throw runners out trying to advance to another bag. They need to back up the infielders when the ball gets hit to them, back up fellow outfielders, and back up bases. There is ALWAYS something for them to do. I also want to challenge coaches to let the youth softball players know how important outfielders are. I know I'm not the first person to say this, nor will I be the last, but outfielders are the last line of defense. Missing a ball in the infield will hurt you; missing a ball in the outfield will kill you. That means when an infielder makes an error the hitter usually only gets to first base. When an outfielder makes an error the hitter can get to second, third, or even all the way home.

There are two main aspects that I feel make up the mindset of an outfielder. First is the confidence that you will catch every ball hit your way. You must make the hitter believe she cannot get anything past you by proving she can't. Your teammates coaches, opponents, and fans must believe you will do everything in your power to make a play, even if it means diving for a ball out of reach. You should train with the same mindset you would have on game day. You have to take that dive in practice so when game time comes, you can do it without thinking and without fear.

The second aspect is to ALWAYS have your pitcher's back. Your pitcher works her butt off to throw the perfect pitch to get the batter out. If a flyable is hit, it is the outfielder's job to make the catch and complete the play. The trust between a pitcher and outfielder is an amazing thing. For ex., when she knows you will go over, through, or around the fence to catch the ball, you know she is going to throw a pitch to give you the best chance to make a play.

Is it realistic that you will catch everything in the outfield? No, but having the right mindset will go a long way to achieving this goal. You have to take ownership of the field and let yourself and everyone know that it belongs to you.

About Laura Berg

Laura Berg is the current head coach for the Oregon State Beavers softball program, a post she has held since 2012. Berg had an illustrious playing career at Fresno State University, where she led the team to a Women's College World Series title and still holds the school records for hits, triples, and runs scored. She was selected to play with Team USA in 1994. During her international career, she helped the team win 11 medals, 10 of which were gold medals, between the Olympics, ISF Women's World Championship, and Pan-American Games. She is also the only member of Team USA to play in all four Olympic games in which softball was a participant. Her efforts earned her Olympic Hall of Fame honors in 2012.

Lisa Iancin

"The Moment"

The point of contact of a bat hitting a ball takes place in a moment. The measurable amount of time passing is so quick, it is easy to overlook all of the precise steps taken in order for the collision to happen. Your last strikeout and previous home run both have something in common; they are in the past. What you bring to this moment will always come back and how you perceive this moment will outlast.

I see the swing to have three aspects; the Physical Aspect, the Mental Aspect, and the Emotional Aspect. Each aspect has many parts, such as keeping your elbows high, striding to even, and extension through the zone. These are all elements of the physicality of our swing. The mental has more to do with which pitch is "my" pitch right now, as the count continues to change. Knowing that I will have a tight strike zone if the count is 0-0, versus a larger strike zone on a 3-2 count. The zone contracts and expands pitch by pitch, and staying aware of that helps our mental preparedness to swing at better pitches. The Emotional Aspect of our swing is what I want talk about now. It is so important, yet often a topic that isn't covered because we know that we have to teach the other two aspects first. You can't tell a hitter to make an adjustment at the plate if they don't know how to physically do it. Similarly, you can't tell them to be a smart hitter, if they have no understanding of what they should be swinging at. Therefore the first two aspects of the swing demand so much time, care, and attention. Often enough, we spend most of our efforts coaching these first two aspects. We want to be good coaches so we go online and research video hitting drills on YouTube. We bring our knowledge to practice and set up tee stations to develop correct physical movement. We scout pitchers by watching video of past games so we can mentally plan on what to swing at. However, come game time, we still have a hard go at it because something is off, something is still missing. It is at this time when as a coach you have to ask yourself if you remembered to coach the emotional aspect of the swing.

What is the emotional aspect of the swing? Here is an example I just ran into. It's mid March in the Northeast and we're getting close to season. All winter I've been training a young hitter who is a student of the game. She likes learning and I can tell she probably gets good grades in school. Yet for some reason this week she is off and hitting everything straight down into the ground. Quickly, I find the root of the issue and notice she isn't coiling her hands back during the load phase of her swing. For this reason, she can't completely get to where she's aiming because her range of motion is limited. I tell her to coil her wrists back more towards the catcher's opposite shin guard. She tries but doesn't quite get there. Finally I ask her why is it she can't get her hands to that spot. She says that in high school practice, they are taking cuts off the machine and all of the balls are old so most of the pitches are wild. Therefore, they have to rush hitters through to make up for lost time. When the pitches are coming in one after another too quickly, she feels like she doesn't have enough time for her complete swing to take place, so she has adjusted by cutting her swing short. As a result, she has enough time to make contact with the ball, but there is no power and everything is being hit low. The emotion of fear of being late was transferring into our hitting lesson. Even though we were working off the tee and there was plenty of time, that emotion had carried over. At this moment, I had to break from talking about the physical aspect of her swing and address the emotional side since that appeared as the root of her hitting issue. Instead of repeating myself about coiling her hands, I told her to trust her hands because she has plenty of bat speed. I reminded her that there was not a pitcher at any high school in her area that possessed enough speed to blow one by her. To ease the fear of being late, I told her to start her swing earlier. Instantly, her swing came back to life and she was driving the ball with height again. In this instance, we needed to address the emotional aspect of her swing. This is an elementary example that occurred with a youth hitter, yet the transference of our emotions into the swing can also take place at the collegiate and pro levels. Just imagine as the stakes become higher, so does the intensity of our emotions.

I've been called an expert in hitting, someone who can really break down the swing. Yes, I do know the swing because I am forever a student of the game. However I believe the thing that makes me a good teacher has more to do with how I relate to kids. I had a parent joke with me one time and say that I must have a degree in child psychology. Clearly I don't, but I do think the years of experience training youth players has given me insight on how to get through to them. Also the years of playing ball from youth to college, into my own professional career means that I can likely relate to just about any frustration, celebration, or emotion that a young player is now having to deal with. Drawing back is where the expertise comes from, the rest is listening.

Beyond that, there are divergent learning styles. Each hitter is different and has a unique way of seeing the world and building their interpretations of it. Some are visual learners and need to see you do the drill correctly before they can do it. Other players are intellectual learners and need each step broken down into numerical data so they can relate it to the same success they feel after a good grade in math class. I find myself using more visual apps with them like Coach's Eye or the Zepp. Some players don't need to think, they just do it. Often times, those players don't need a lot of instruction on how to hit the ball, but just alignment so they keep it in fair territory. These are examples of different learning styles however we should also be aware of individual temperaments within a swing.

For example, some hitters can't hit through the infield because their swing is too slow. They don't know how to swing hard and explode through the ball because they are not aggressive by nature. Instead, they are timid, shy, or afraid of swinging at the wrong pitch. Strike three passes by and they are caught looking! For this hitter, I may have to teach her how to talk smack back to the pitcher, silently of course as the umpire is standing right there. Other players have plenty of aggressive energy, confidence, and talent but they can't handle failure. They swing early at the first pitch and it is all downhill from there. Now she's swinging at everything and driving it all foul until she is deep in the count and going after bad pitches. In this case, ambition has us chasing our own tail. For this kid, I tell her that every time she throws her helmet or rolls her eyes, the pitcher loves it. She just set a trap for you and you are walking right into it. For this temperament, I teach a balance of humility and the importance of staying humble to the game. If you lose sight of the adjustment you need to make, it can be a long season.

When it comes down to it, there is a point when we need to recognize the psychological elements of each player's game. Every player and every team is different, however we all have a common goal of winning. In order to do that, we need to find ways to shape our weaknesses into strengths. We need to shift our outlook so that challenges are worth facing because victory is worth tasting. As coaches we need to know our players and know how to get through to them to bring the best out of them. Can you pinpoint their unique learning style and know what motivates them? Or is your coaching style more about you than them? Of course I believe in consistency and administering discipline as positive and necessary coaching traits. I'm just saying, we need to know our players to know how to make them better. Yelling the correct base to throw to from the dugout isn't always the best method of creating smart and independent players. There are times when we need to listen to them to know what their hang-ups are. Back in my college coaching days, we would have quarterly player meetings. Players would come in the office and have individual time to sit and talk with the coaches. This offered a separate setting from group practice on the field. Every now and then, this is a good way to learn about each player's strengths, weaknesses, and motivations so that you figure how to best develop them.

If we want to win it all, we need to know that our players are ready for their moment when it shows up in the game. They chose to play one of the few team sports that offer each player their very own personal moment. A lot happens in a softball game. Players are fielding out on defense, running the bases, or sitting in the dugout spitting out sunflower seeds. Yet somewhere in that span of a seven inning game, most players will go up to bat. This is every hitter's moment, in which they stand in the box alone. When that player is holding the bat neither you coaching at third base nor their parents have a say in what happens next. Do you think they are ready for their moment? How do you think each of your players feel about this moment? Does all of the pressure and attention get to them? Now that everyone has their eyes on them, do they love this moment or would they rather press fast forward to their teammate's at-bat?

For this moment, you need to have coached confidence into your players. In the end, that's all you really can do. Help them value both failure and triumph as they are interrelated. This is their moment in which no one tells them what to do. In this millisecond moment as they decipher between ball or strike, they are not seeking permission, it is now their choice. Remember the Emotional Aspect of hitting and how it can shape the mental and physical. Therefore, let's develop the emotional. How do they perceive challenges? Teach them that challenges are not to be avoided, but to be perceived as opportunity. In other words, we don't need to shy away from pressure or pretend it doesn't exist. We need to welcome pressure and use it as fuel to overcome our challenges. If you can coach a kid to welcome their pressure moment on the field, you've already won. For these lessons won't leave them after the game does, their moment will show up again.

About Lisa Iancin

Lisa Iancin, "LI", competed in National Pro Fastpitch (NPF) for 5 seasons, winning a national championship in 2004 with the New York/ New Jersey Juggernaut and again in 2006 with the New England Riptide. In 2005, Iancin was named the NPF Defensive Player of the Year and she played shortstop, second base, and third base.

Lisa earned a full scholarship to the University of California, Berkeley. Among her accolades as a Golden Bear are First Team All-Pac 10 and back-to-back appearances at the Women's College World Series in 1999 and 2000. Iancin had the opportunity to play internationally as well for Team Bussolengo, Italy in 2001.

From 2006-2009, Iancin served as the Assistant Softball Coach at the George Washington University where she concurrently completed a Masters in Tourism Administration with an emphasis in Sports Management. In 2010, Iancin was named the Assistant General Manager of the Tennessee Diamonds and the Director of Corporate Partnerships in 2013 for the NY/NJ Comets. Iancin was also the Marketing/Instruction/ Public Relations Coordinator of the Jennie Finch Softball Academy – Diamond Nation in Flemington, New Jersey.

Owner and Head Trainer of LI Softball Academy in Jersey City, NJ, Iancin has over 10 years' experience as a fastpitch softball instructor and team clinician. LI is dedicated to raising the platform that female professional athletes stand on, and hence serves as a sports marketing representative and photographer at PhotosByLI.com.

Meagan Denny-White

"Pitching with a Purpose"

The transformation from being a thrower to a pitcher is not an easy one. I could throw a softball 70 + MPH. So the first half of my career I could throw a fastball, curveball and then a riseball and that batter was on the bench. My physical game made confidence come very easy. Confidence pretty much summed up my mental game. I didn't care who was up to bat or even what the count was. I knew whatever the situation was I was going to win without a single doubt. The next step of my career was not so simple. In college the game got a little more complicated.

Physically there is no one right way for every pitcher. Every pitcher has her own physical style and strengths. But the physical game is not what makes her. A pitchers mental game is what makes her or breaks her. It was not until the end of my playing career that I developed my strongest mental game. I learned how to keep the game simple. Before, I was so focused on my opponent's strengths and weaknesses that I sometimes forgot to be confident in my own strengths.

 I found myself playing to their game and not my own. The harder I tried to pitch to their weaknesses and not to my strengths I did not perform well. I had mental overload. All of this lead to doubting myself, worrying about how everyone thought about how terrible I was doing. The harder I tried the worse it got. I was not thinking effectively. Now not only had I lost faith in myself but my team had as well. That was the most heart-breaking thing of all.

I finally got to the point where I made the decision to change my way of thinking during the game. I decided to go back to keeping it simple and pitching smart. At this point I simply did not care who was up to bat anymore because I knew I am a great pitcher and anything I throw is going to be difficult for them to hit. By focusing on how to effectively use my strengths I became more confident. When a pitcher has confidence in herself it shows in her presence. That confident presence is contagious to your team and intimidating to your opponents.

To help get your mind right pitch-to-pitch you have to establish a routine between pitches. Between pitches you only have 10 seconds to be ready to throw the next pitch. In that short amount of time you have to create a positive approach for the next pitch. If the last pitch did not turn out the way you wanted it to, for example if you gave up a hit, you hit the batter, it was close but the umpire called a ball or if you just flat out missed your spot you don't have enough time to get upset and frustrated. All that negative energy is setting you back from getting to your positive approach for the next pitch. Just because the last pitch didn't work the way you originally planned for it to does not mean it didn't serve a purpose. You just have to find out how to make all of your pitches in an at bat to work together to ultimately get the batter out.

Your mental routine should start by **taking a deep breath**. Relax your mind and body in order to get focused. Then you have to know the **PURPOSE** of the pitch. For example, if you have a 0-0 count that pitch is to get ahead. If you have a 1-2 count that pitch's purpose is to be believable to the batter but hard for her to hit it and ultimately win the count by striking her out, getting her to ground out or pop it up so that the play is easy for the defense.

The next step in your mental routine should be to know the **PROCESS**, which means knowing **HOW** to make that that pitch fulfill its purpose. You must know where to throw the pitch. You don't want to throw a 0-2 pitch anywhere close to the corner of the plate. You also have to know what your body needs to do in order to throw each pitch. The body works differently for a curve ball than it does a rise ball. And with a screw ball your body positioning to throw this pitch is off the power line. Each pitch calls for its own proper mechanics. You should know how to throw each pitch properly.

The last step in your routine before you start your motion is to **COMMIT** to the pitch. If you don't have full trust in your pitch then it's doomed. If there is any doubt at all don't throw the pitch, shake it off and get another pitch, step off call time out to talk to your catcher, or just simply fake your confidence. Fake it till you make it.

So as you see there is absolutely no time to think about what you're doing wrong, how bad the umpire is, or knowing every single thing about each batter. Pitchers tend to overload their heads with unnecessary information that blankets the important information like the PURPOSE, PROCESS, and your COMMITMENT to the pitch in order to make the pitch as successful as you can. When you get off track with this routine you need to stay patient, find the positive in the situation and stay persistent with your routine. The only thing you can control in this game is your attitude and your effort. This routine will help you stay focused on the controllables, not the uncontrollables, and keep the game simple.

About Meagan Denny-White

Meagan Denny-White has a long list of accomplishments both as a player and a coach. She was a part of 2 championship teams at Crowley High School and was also on the USA Junior National Team, where she helped the team win Silver in the Junior World Championships. Denny-White continued her career at the University of Texas where she is third all time in innings pitched, wins, appearances, starts, complete games, shutouts, and strikeouts. Her career did not stop in Austin; she moved on to the professional ranks where she played on the Pro Fastpitch Xtreme Tour from 2008-2011. Her playing career ended in 2012 with the Chicago Bandits of the NPF. Meagan lead the Southwest Christian Lady Eagles to their first district championship and state tournament where they were TAPPS State runner up in 2012. She moved on to serve as pitching coach at The University of Texas Arlington from 2012-2014. Today, Denny-White is a private pitching instructor in Midlothian, Texas.

Michele Martin Diltz

"Competitive Training"

Training for the physical development of the softball player is a very important part of building a well-rounded athlete; however, finding time and space to train your athletes is usually the hardest part. Along with time and space there is also the stigma that training is not fun and the athletes don't want to do it. You can change their attitude so that the athletes have a "get to" train vs. "have to" train mentality. By using the tool – Competitive Training - you can lead your team through a great training session during practice by masking the "workout" with relays, group activities and games fitting in physical development while they are having fun doing what they love to do – Competing.

Compete

Athletes LOVE to compete. The definition of "athlete: is a person who *competes* in one or more activities that involves physical strength, speed and/or endurance." Competition is what makes an athlete want to be an athlete and they will compete at anything. Who can make the most paper balls into the wastebasket? Who can get to the car the fastest to get the front seat? Who can do the most jumping jacks? Who can hold the plank for the longest? This drive to win is in all your athletes and when you put them into competitive game-like situations the athletes will be more aggressive and work at a higher intensity than if you just told them to run a 300 yard shuttle. When competing whether as an individual or as a team the athlete will compete at a high level when something is on the line either intrinsically for pride or extrinsically for reward or lack of punishment. The more that the athletes compete there will be a driving force for adaptation and the athlete will learn how to adapt to the pressure and game-like intensity.

Get that Extra Boost

Incorporating competitive training into practice or even your normal training session can be fun and entertaining and will give your athletes that little extra boost to finish strong. Competitive Training can be completed with little to no equipment, with limited space, in a small amount of time and during every practice but should not replace a true training sessions. These activities can be placed at the beginning of practice or training session to get the competitive energy flowing. It can also be placed at the end of practice or training session so that you can send the athlete's home remembering what it feels like to compete. These competitions can be rewarded by either punishment for the losers, reward for the winner or for pride. Competitive training activities or games can be completed by an individual athlete or small even groups.

Individuals

An individual athlete will be competing against themself or their teammates. For the best results the activity should be a single max effort for 1 round. By competing against self it can replicate what everyday practice should be, always trying to give the best individual effort and to make improvements so the team is better.

Group

When competing in a team or in group the competition will encourage cooperation, concentration, coordination and creativity amongst athletes. Splitting the team into 3 – 5 athlete groups to compete as a team will allow more involvement and less standing around. The competitive activities or games can be put into best 2 out of 3 formats.

Competitive Training Activities

Below are 5 examples of competitive training exercises that can be completed either as an individual or in groups. Know that these are competitive training activities to get you thinking and that there are an unlimited number of activities that could be used to get your team competing.

i.   Jump Rope: Equipment Needed – Jump Ropes, Stopwatch

Single	Goal
Beginner	How many jumps can you complete with 2 feet without messing up? (record #)
Intermed	How long to complete 50 continuous jumps on 2 feet without messing up? (record time)
Advanced	How many Double Unders can you complete without messing up? (record #)

Group	Goal
Beginner	How many jumps can the team complete with 2 feet without messing up in a relay against other groups? Example – team of 4 – Athlete 1 goes till mess up, then athlete 2, athlete 3, athlete 4 (the winning team will have the most completed reps)
Intermed	How long for the group to complete 50 continuous jumps on 2 feet without messing up each? Example – team of 4 – Stopwatch starts when athlete 1 begins jumping on completion of 50 continuous reps the jump rope will be passed to athlete 2, then athlete 3, then athlete 4. At completion of athlete 4 the stopwatch is stopped. (the winning team will have the fastest time)
Advanced	Double Unders Relay - Which group can complete 5 -4-3-2-1 Double Unders the fastest without messing up? Example – team of 4 – On command "go" athlete 1 completes 5 continuous double unders passing jump rope to athlete 2, then onto athlete 3, and athlete 4. Returning to athlete 1 to complete 4 double unders, then athlete 2, athlete 3, athlete 4. Back to athlete 1 for 3 doubles unders following down the line till athlete 4 completes 1 double under. (the winning team will complete it the fastest)

ii. **Burpees:** Equipment Needed – Stopwatch

Single	Goal
	Complete 25 Burpees for time (record #)

iii. **Push-ups:** Equipment Needed – none

Single	Goal
	Complete max number of push-ups.

Group	Goal
	Push-Up Relay: Which group can complete 5-4-3-2-1 Push-ups the fastest? Example – team of 4 - On command "go" athlete 1 completes 5 push-ups while the rest of the team is holding plank then athlete 2, then onto athlete 3, and athlete 4. Returning to athlete 1 to complete 4 push-ups through the team for all 4 reps, then 3reps, then 2 reps, then 1rep. If one player has to rest the whole team rests and continues when the whole team is either doing push-ups or planking. The relay is complete when athlete 4 completes the last push-up. (the winning team will complete it the fastest)

iv. Leg Circuits: Equipment Needed - stopwatch

Single	Goal
	Complete 20 body weight squats, 10 each leg alternating lunges, 10 Squat Jumps for time.

Group	Goal
	Leg Circuit Relay: Which group can complete 20 body weight squats, 10 each leg alternating lunges and 10 Squats jumps the fastest?
	Example – team of 4 - On command "go" athlete 1 completes 20 body weight squats then athlete 2, then onto athlete 3, and athlete 4. Returning to athlete 1 to complete 10 each leg alternating lunges, then onto athlete 2, athlete 3 and athlete 4. Back to athlete 1 to complete 10 squats jumps, then onto athlete 2, 3, and 4. The relay is complete when athlete 4 completes the last squat jumps. (the winning team will complete it the fastest)

v. Broad Jumps: Equipment Needed – measuring tape or marker

Single	Goal
	Complete a standing broad jump to max distance.

Group	Goal

Broad Jump Relay: Which group can complete the most distance in 2 minutes worth of work.

Example – team of 4 - On command "go" athlete 1 completes a standing max broad jump then athlete 2 where athlete 1 landed completes standing max broad jump , then onto athlete 3 where athlete 2 landed completes standing max broad jump, and athlete 4 completes a standing max broad jump where athlete 3 landed rotating through until the completion of time. (the winning team will accumulate the most distance covered)

Conclusion:

An athlete is a person who competes so you as the coach can take advantage of that drive and start increasing the level of training intensity by incorporating competitive training into your daily practice and training sessions. A rising tide lifts all boats and adaptation of the athlete physically and mentally from competing will elevate your team one step closer to the end goal.

About Michele Martin Diltz

Michele Martin Diltz (NSCA – CPT, CSCS, CSCCa – SCCC) has been the Strength and Conditioning Coach for The University of Alabama softball and women's golf teams since 2005. During this time she has had the opportunity to be part of a NCAA Softball National Championship

(2012) and 5 SEC Softball Championships as well as a NCAA Golf National Championship (2012) and 2 SEC Woman's Golf Championship. Michelle holds a B.S. in Kinesiology from Texas Woman's University, where she played outfield for the Pioneer softball team as well she holds a M.S in Sports Physiology from Texas A&M University. Michelle believes that high forces and rapid loading are an inherent fact of sports, and the role of the strength and conditioning coach is to systematically prepare the athletes to handle these forces in order to reduce the chance of injury while improving performance.

Mitch Alexander

"Pressure Cooker"

Most of the drills coaches run in practices don't do a very good job of simulating real game pressure and emotions. We are great at setting up drills for fielding and drills for throwing, but players typically master these drills fairly quickly, especially at the older levels. Since we are always looking for ways to challenge and improve our players, I was looking for a new drill to better simulate the pressure and emotions felt in real game situations. I came across a drill we call the "Pressure Cooker". Unfortunately, I don't know who created it, but it's a great drill. We have modified it from the original to form "Pressure Cooker" and "Pressure Cooker 2," which incorporates even more realism and works on even more skills.

Both drills can be performed indoors or outdoors. Very little equipment is needed for these drills: a bucket of balls, an empty bucket, bases, and three optional small cones. These drills can be run with just one coach, or with as many as four coaches. A minimum of three players is required to run this drill, and since it's a quick running drill, there is no practical maximum. This drill should be appropriate for 9 year olds through college level.

In the most basic version, you create two "teams." The first team wears batting helmets and lines up behind home plate. The second team lines up behind 2nd base with their gloves and defensive facemasks if they wear them. The first fielder in line takes their position on 2nd base using good form to defend against a base runner with a non-force tag out. Another fielder, takes their position on third base. The coach places three softballs on the third base foul line: the first is 5 feet from third base towards home plate, the second is 10 feet, and the third is 15 feet. The optional cones can be placed at these intervals to prevent the ball spacing from changing distances between rounds.

The first runner on the running team takes up a batting stance at home plate without a bat. Since there are two teams competing here, there are two different objectives. When the coach blows a whistle, or shouts, "GO" the runner will drop their arms from holding their imaginary bat, stay low coming out of the batter's box, sprint down the first base foul line, staying to the right of the line in the runner's lane. The runner needs to make a good turn hitting the inside left part of the first base bag and continue on to second base. If you are doing this drill outside, you can optionally add sliding or popup slides into the drill.

For the fielding team, when the coach shouts "GO" the fielder on third base runs to the first ball and then throws it to second base. The second baseman must catch the ball and place it in the empty bucket. The third baseman runs to the second ball and repeats, and finally repeats with the third ball. The objective is for the runner to beat out the final throw of the third ball. If they do, the running team is awarded a point. If the fielding team gets the third ball in the bucket before the runner touches second base, they are awarded a point. After the 3 ball round is over, the player on third base goes to the end of the line at second base, and the player on second base rotates to third base.

Additional coaches can be added to this drill. Place a coach 6 feet away from home plate down the foul line just to the right of the running lane with an arm or swimming pool noodle outstretched at shoulder height. The batter/runner needs to stay low coming out of the box in a sprint and not touch the arm or noodle. Another coach can be placed standing on first base to ensure the batter/runner only hits the left inside portion of the bag and makes an efficient turn at first base.

In "Pressure Cooker 2," we add pitching and hitting. A pitcher, or coach at the younger levels, throws batting practice style pitches (walkthroughs, or other type of pitch at 75% speed). This time the batter uses a bat and tries to hit the ball up the middle. Having a pass-through screen is great for these, especially if a coach is pitching from twenty feet out. Many of the batted balls should hit the screen at this distance. Instead of the coach starting the drill by shouting "GO," this time the drill starts when the bat hits the ball. The players on line at second base can be placed in the outfield to field the balls being batted out. If you have another spare empty bucket place it near the center fielder to collect the batted balls. You can add the additional coaches on the running lane and at first base as well.

Have each fielder run through the drill two times and then switch sides. We usually have each team play each side twice so that each fielder gets 4 repetitions. If your fielders consistently miss making good throws, keep working the drill with more reps. Keep a tally of each team's score and see who won at the end of the competition.

Coaches should pay attention to many different aspects of this drill. Make sure the fielders are showing ready position. Coach the players on how to field a static ball, since the throw is from down the third base foul line to second base, the fielder needs to change position to make the throw accurately. Coming around the ball in a type of circular motion allows the fielder to quickly field the ball and be setup in a position to make the throw to second base. A quick accurate throw is required. For the runners, make sure they are getting out of the batter's box quickly, staying low in a sprint, making efficient turns and not overrunning second base.

If your fielders are consistently winning the competition, increase the difficulty by moving the balls closer to home plate. You can even practice this drill by placing the balls on the base-path between second and third bases, or on fielding the bunt by putting the three balls in a semicircle 4 feet out in front of home plate or in a straight line from home plate to the pitcher's circle and move your fielder from third base to first base. In this case, you may want to use safety balls, as runners may get hit in the back under the pressure of the drill.

This is a great drill that allows players to become more confident playing under pressure. The kind of pressure they have in real games. When you first start using this drill, you will find that the fielders try to rush the throw under pressure, and miss hitting the second baseman with inaccurate throws. Even your best arms will have issues running this drill the first few times. Runners will run through second base, in which case, if all the balls are in the bucket, they are out. Try running this drill at the end of practice, as it's a great exercise that your players will have fun with, and it will motivate them to work hard at your next practice.

About Mitch Alexander

Mitch Alexander is the CIO for a major electronics company and coaches both Little League and Travel softball teams and is currently completing his PhD. He is a certified SUNY, ASA, and Double Goal Coach. His wife, Marie was one of the first female student athletes in the country to play Little League softball after Title IX was passed and played in the first Little League Softball World Series. Over the years, both have managed teams together and helped spark a love for softball in their student athletes. In his spare time, Mitch designs websites for fastpitch teams and businesses and can be reached at mitchalexander@optonline.net.

Rita Lynn Gilman

"Double Ball Drills"

The double ball is a tool pitchers can use to help create tight spin. It is simple to use and equally as easy to make; all you need are two softballs, electrical tape, and adhesive. Wrap a thin piece of electrical tape around each ball. Next adhere the two balls together. Let the adhesive set up and you are ready to go! If you would like to watch a video on how to use it effectively, visit www.softballpitchingtools.com.

1. **Fastball**

   Flips: Prop the double ball up in your finger pads so the two balls are stacked upright. Find your fastball grip on the bottom ball. Thumb should be opposite the middle finger. Using your fingers and wrist in a snapping action, flip the double ball end over end as fast as possible. This creates tight topspin for the fastball and drop ball.

   Rolls: Lay the double ball flat in your hand with middle finger in the gap below the balls and with thumb in the gap above the balls. Using your fingers and wrist in a snapping action, roll the double ball off your fingertips. Your goal is fast spin while keeping the double ball level.

   5 drills with the "roll" grip:
   Self flip
   High self flip

High self windmill

Half toss to catcher at 15 feet

Windmill to catcher and progress further back

2. **Backhand Change-Up**

Gripping the bottom ball, prop the double ball up behind your hip, arm fully extended with back of hand leading. Swing arm in front of body and flip the double ball backwards as fast as possible. This creates backspin. Catch in pitching hand for additional dexterity work.

Half toss to a catcher at 15 feet

Repeat the two tosses above with the roll grip. Keep the double ball level for perfect backspin.

3. **Curve Ball**

Grip the bottom ball and hold double ball below waist with wrist cupped up. Balls will be stacked up. Just like snapping your fingers, twist the double ball like a curve. If your side spin is perfect, the double ball will remain perfectly upright and will spin tightly. This is very difficult at first!!

6 Curve Ball Drills:

Self spin

High self spin

Half toss to self

Windmill to self
Half toss to catcher at 5 feet
Windmill to catcher at 10 feet

4. **Rise Ball**

Get your grip on the bottom ball with the two balls stacked straight up in front of your hip. Fingers will start behind the ball. Flip the double ball end over end by driving the bottom ball under and up. Flip to yourself and then 10 feet to your catcher.

Hold the double ball parallel to the ground with the top ball pointing away from your hip. Start with double ball below waist with fingers under the ball. Just like snapping your fingers, twist the double ball like a rise. If your backspin is perfect, the double ball will remain perfectly level and will spin tightly. This is very challenging!!! Stick with it until perfect!!

6 Rise Ball Drills:
Self spin
High self spin
Half toss to self
Windmill to self
Half toss to catcher at 5 feet
Windmill to catcher at 10 feet

5. **<u>Wrist/Finger Roller</u>**

Tie a 4 foot rope around the middle of the double ball. Attach a 2.5-5 pound weight to the bottom of the rope. With elbows at your sides and arms at a 90 degree angle, grip both softballs in your fingertips. Twist the softballs with your fingertips until the weight winds all the way up. Repeat in opposite direction for a fantastic finger, wrist and forearm workout that looks a lot like your riseball action!!!

About Rita Lynn Gilman

Considered the premiere fastpitch softball pitching instructor in the Richmond, Virginia area, Rita Lynn has influenced the careers of many outstanding pitchers in over 28 years of instruction, including the 2014 USA Softball National Player of the Year, Florida State's Lacey Waldrop since age 10 and 2014 2nd-Team All-American Jailyn Ford of James Madison University since age 10.

Rita Lynn is a full-time pitching instructor at her training center on her family farm in Hanover County, Va. A member of the National Fastpitch Coaches Association, she has attended the NFCA Convention and Advanced Pitching Analysis Coaches College several times.

You can find Rita Lynn's popular DVD's and unique pitching training tools on her website: www.softballpitchingtools.com

Rob Crews

"7 Phases of Visual Mechanics"

The one component in the hitting process most under taught is definitely the visual process. How to improve visual hitting mechanics is something that has eluded the most innovative hitting coaches and to this day remains somewhat of a mystery.

Vision Training as an industry is something that more and more teams and individuals are seeking but most are not very consistent with. I believe that education is key. The proper understanding of the visual process as it relates to performance, especially hitting, is crucial and necessary for the evolution of the game; crucial to evolution of development in hitting as we know it and performance in general.

So the questions remain: Is hitting a mental or physical process? What percentage of the hitting process is mental/visual? How can we get our young hitters to embrace vision training in the developmental process? This is something I have dedicated my entire coaching life to and yet I have only scratched the surface.

This is a question I always ask my hitters -as a coach you should ask this question to your teams. As a player, you should ask yourself this question.

Question: Is the hitting process more mental or physical? What percentage of it is mental/visual?

So I think we would all agree that more than 70 percent of the hitting process is mental/visual?

Most hitters want to come to practice and do something physical. They want to swing and swing and swing some more. If you make the training program too cerebral, the sport itself can become a turnoff to most young hitters. Therefore, finding an effective and efficient way to balance how we implement vision training into the daily routine of a hitter can be a challenge. I believe that the knowledge of how the visual system of human performance works or the process of how hitters visually ascertain visual data, and finding creative ways to improve and maintain it are major factors of how hitting can and will evolve.

I have outlined 7 phases of the visual process – a process that precedes the swing and has a direct effect on the swing. I have always maintained that the swing itself is a result of what we see and how we process it. When we attempt to develop hitters without considering how they visually process information, we are doing them a huge disservice. Those 7 phases go a little something like this:

Note: I may use the word "file" and "pitch" interchangeably

1. Create file

The process of hitting, especially at a high-level, begins with establishing a database of files, or pitches, that you the hitter has seen over the course of your career. I call it *experiential memory* or simply *files*. The players with the most files will undoubtedly recognize pitches much sooner and faster. To take it a step further, the players with the most files versus better pitching, will have a better database than players with tons of files versus mediocre pitching.

2. Record a file

There are some hitters who may have a tougher time recording the files they have created, or pitches they have seen. These hitters are unable to adjust from pitch to pitch. A perfect example is a hitter that gets a pitch blown by them on the first pitch and then fails to catch up with that same pitch when they see it again for a second time in as many pitches. The bottom line is, a high-level player has a responsibility to store, recognize, recall, and match files (pitches) and do so at a high speed.

3. Store a file

Storing files is about memory. Filing those 1st inning change -ups for future recall in the 4th inning or when you see that same pitcher or pitch later in the season.

4. Recognize a file ·

Recognition comes down to 2 questions -have you seen this before and how frequently have you seen it? It is impossible to recognize something you haven't already seen? And the more you see it, the faster you can recognize it. Hence, more than 60 percent of the MLB draft comes from warmer states where hitters play more baseball and see more pitches. Those hitters more than likely have more files stored. File storage-recognition usually translates into success, specifically at higher levels of play. Of course there will be exceptions, we are talking about developing normal people into elite level hitters.

5. Recall a file

Recollection is all about file retrieval. As a hitter, I am virtually taking the pitches I have seen in the past and matching them with the pitch

I see in the present, in order to predict what is about to happen in the future. And by the way, I am (6) **Matching the Files** in less than a half a second. The players who are able to do this the fastest, can play at higher levels. The players who can only do this at certain speeds, are limited in how high a level they can play. Once the game speeds up, the speed in which individuals can process visual information becomes exposed. This is where mechanics break down. So if you wondered why certain players under-perform against faster pitching, it is mostly because eyes and brain cannot work together fast enough to (7) **Coordinate the Correct Response**.

The swing or the coordination of the proper response is where most hitting development begins and ends. The truth is that most hitters have great swings but can't hit, or even worse, hitters have strong and fast swings that are late - late due to visual mis-information.

These are your 7 Phases of Visual Performance Mechanics. If you missed 6 and 7, you will find them hidden inside number 5.

About Rob Crews

There is a long list of players and programs Rob has had a major influence on. Some of the top baseball and softball prospects from the Northeast, from Youth, Collegiate, Professional and Olympic level, and college teams in the Pac-10, SEC, Big West, C-USA, CAA, MEAC, ACC, and Atlantic Ten conferences. Current and past companies Rob has consulted in the areas of business development
are SKLZ, T2Motion, Nokona, Insignia Athletics, Sports195, Hittinguru.

Rob has and currently supports a host of different travel organizations ranging in age groups from 9U-18U. In the summer of 2010, Rob Crews served as Assistant and Hitting Coach for the USSSA Pride, the 2010 National Pro Fastpitch Champions. Rob has also consulted the Venezuelan National Softball Team and its coaching staff in the areas of hitting, mental focus, and visual strategies for pitch recognition. Facilities and training centers where Rob can be found are 4D Sports (Southern NY), Fastpitch Nation (Conn), and A.M.P. (Long Island, NY). Rob is the author of the books, COMPLETE GAME (2006) and SWAG 101 (2013), mental skills publications for improving in-game focus and confidence.

Find more at www.Complete-Game.com

Shannon McDougall

"Periodization – The Yearly Training Plan"

The purpose of this chapter is to try to simplify one of the most complicated and intimidating concepts in coaching that can have the biggest impact on your season regardless of your team's age or skill level. This is a very small sample of a tool that consists of so much more than what is presented here. Periodization, or a yearly training plan, is essentially a plan for success, which considers your athlete's developmental stage. It begins with an end in mind and works backwards to ensure that you have done all you can to help your team.

It starts with breaking up your season into parts, called phases, which is what we will discuss in this chapter. Each phase of your plan has a specific purpose leading up to and through your most important tournament of the season.

A Yearly Training Plan will provide:

- A mental training plan that builds a solid foundation of basic mental skills and strategies.

- A physical training plan.
- A technical and tactical training plan that solidifies fundamental skills and refines advanced skills depending on the readiness of your athletes.
- A plan for nutrition and hydration while learning how to maximize energy levels and recovery.
- A plan using environmental strategies that will enable the athletes to deal with varying weather conditions and altitude changes.

Phases of the Yearly Training Plan for Softball

General Preparation Phase (Approximately 20 Weeks) -

Refining of technical and evaluation of tactical skills is mostly done during this phase. The ability to execute basic fundamental skills under various conditions will be the difference when it counts the most.

Mental training skills will give your team the ability to adapt to those various conditions mentioned and if not already done, should be introduced here. Self-regulation, emotional control, and stress management are all skills that can be introduced and developed during this phase, but not necessarily requiring competition to develop. Team cohesion is also crucial, as the group will be spending a large amount of time together throughout the season.

Physical training in the form of anatomical adaptation during this phase will build the foundation for further strength and power training during the next phases. Building an aerobic base as well as general endurance training will assist with recovery during tournaments.

It is important that athletes learn at least a general awareness of nutrition and how it will affect their energy levels and ability to recover during tournaments. Without proper fuel, the ability to do work will diminish and the best results will not be possible. In addition, hydration should become a habit to prevent dehydration and heat stroke.

Specific Preparation Phase (Approximately 6 Weeks) -

Utilizing mental training skills that are learned in the General Preparation Phase in daily life will allow athletes to more easily transfer their skills to the field. Simply being familiar and aware is a start; deliberately using mental skills for emotional control, stress management, distraction control, and mental rehearsal in various conditions will assist with the transfer.

Strength training should now be the focus for physical training. Softball is a power sport which requires maximum strength in skills such as throwing and hitting.

Maintaining fundamental technical and tactical skills should be done by creating as many game situations as possible. This will be difficult as the season has not started yet. You will need to be creative and include the athletes in the planning. Integrating mental skills to tactical performance will be done during these game specific sessions.

Pre-Competition Phase (4 Weeks) -

Time to get ready for competition. Implementing new tactics and refining them during exhibition games will be easy having a solid foundation of basic technical and tactical skills

Focus on the evaluation of ability to control emotions in competitive situations during exhibition games and tournaments. Athletes begin devising a preparation plan for competition and game readiness (consider pre-game routines, etc.) while maintaining good mental training abilities through self-evaluation and refining of skills. Use mental skills to deal with distractions and to deal with stress management.

Competitive Phase: (14 Weeks) -

Specific biomotor abilities will be the physical focus during this phase. Anaerobic lactic and alactic training, speed and agility will be trained using sport specific activities and other aids. Always monitor nutritional intake and hydration during exhibition games and training sessions.

Emotional control and self-regulation strategies are being devised and refined as regular competitions are providing great opportunities to develop and establish game readiness routines.

Integrating mental skills in game situations will assist in the refining of the tools being developed to enhance the goal of perfection during games. Perfecting the technical and tactical components under various conditions will be essential to the team's success.

Promote optimal recovery after training and competitions. Ensure good nutritional principles are followed.

Main Competitive Phase (5 Weeks) -

Time to enjoy the game; it is not the time to change things or introduce new skills and strategies. There is nothing that can be done now to change the preparation that has been done throughout the season.

Maintaining physical and technical / tactical gains developed throughout the season will ensure that the athletes maximize their biomotor potential. Sound mental training skills and strategies that were acquired and refined during previous phases will be the difference when you meet the teams of equal abilities.

Transition Phase (3 Weeks) -

This phase is also known as the off-season. Active rest and fun in other sports is the goal during this phase. Reflecting on the season and the positive results will be the beginning of the training for the following season.

The Plan

In addition to what has been discussed here, there are also Microcycles, which are weekly training plans, and Macrocycles, which are groups of weeks that represent a specific objective for that period of time. A yearly training plan can be as simple or as complicated as you like and the amount of information available is endless through numerous books. A search of Tudor Bompa, who is often regarded as the father of periodization, will provide scientifically sound information for you to apply if you would like to design a detailed plan.

Remember to have fun before, during and after the season. Having a yearly training plan will make the things that are usually stressful seem easy. The most important thing is, to HAVE a plan regardless of the level of play. Enjoy.

About Shannon McDougall

Shannon McDougall has been a softball coach at various ages and levels for over 20 years. She has several certifications and degrees including: Associate Sports Science Degree (Canada), Advanced Coaching Diploma (Canadian NCI), Level 3 Softball Coach (Canada), Softball NCCP Facilitator (Canada), Multisport Facilitator (CAC), Junior Athletes Training Specialist (JATS), Periodization – Strength and Conditioning Expert (P-SCE), Periodization – Planning Specialist (P-PS). Shannon maintains a website designed to aid players and coaches develop to their full potential. Visit www.softballtutor.com to improve today!

Shannon Murray

"Pitcher Mental Toughness"

Now the bases are loaded. The game is in extra innings and there are two outs. For the pitcher, this is the ultimate pressure situation. The count is 3-2. One pitch can make or break this game with a one run lead for the pitcher's team. While the dugouts are roaring and crowds chime in, this pitcher must throw the pitch of a life time. She gets her sign, loads back in the wind up and….STEEERIKE THREE! The game is won! The pitcher went with a rise ball for the swing and miss. Seams sizzling by and a cutting movement so quick you could miss it in a blink created one victorious pitch to win the game; but with so much against her, how did she do it? How did she not crack? What's her secret? A pitcher's greatest weapon going into a game, no matter the skill level, is mental toughness. If they are zoned in, completely focused on the task at hand and carry themselves tall through thick and thin, pitchers are sure to be more successful than if they did none of those things. Pitching requires skill and talent that creates a force that cannot be reckoned with. Mental toughness gives pitchers the edge they need to go in a game and dominate each pitch and each at bat with complete composure.

What does mental toughness mean to a softball pitcher? When a situation arises in which the pitcher is behind or made a mistake, bouncing back and going full force forward with the game as if the mistake didn't happen is mental toughness. Nothing in their body language, words, or tone should indicate that they are affected by what happened. Walking a batter or the batter hitting a home run are events every pitcher tries to avoid, but no one is perfect and it's going to happen eventually. The pitcher must find a way to mentally overcome these and other negative situations. Holding onto the mistakes we make as pitchers will only harm us in the long run. It is one grudge pitchers must learn to let go. If a pitcher lets every little mistake get to them, their whole game will deteriorate. Our entire thought process is consumed by the mistakes we make and we are no longer able to focus on what is going to help the team win. Having mental toughness is not only strong, but selfless. By moving on from walks and home runs, your teammates know that everything is going to be alright and that you are still fighting for them. They see hope in you as a pitcher when they see mental toughness. When it's the 6th inning and the other team scored 2 runs off of a home run, holding your head high communicates to your team that you are in no way giving up. In doing so, this shows leadership qualities to your teammates. Whether pitchers realize it or not, by being on the mound they hold a natural role of leadership. The team looks to them every pitch and every play for what's coming next and the pace of the game. They are dependent upon the pitcher to give them a vote of confidence to continue with unyielding strength. Understanding and taking charge of that leadership role gives pitchers more reason to develop mental toughness by knowing that other people are depending on them. Be mentally tough not just for yourself, but for your teammates as well.

Mental toughness doesn't happen overnight. Like any other skill, mental toughness needs regular practice. Whether you're pitching, hitting, playing a position in the field, or conditioning, pitchers should find any opportunity they can to practice mental toughness. How do pitchers uncover some tricks of the trade to practice this? One way you can start is by taking games one pitch at a time. By focusing on one pitch at a time, the pitcher can take out other elements that will only clog her mind in that moment. In that instance of the game the pitcher is only focused on executing that pitch. The more mental obstructions, the harder it is to be mentally tough. Having a short memory can also increase mental toughness. As pitchers, it might be instinct to think about what you did wrong and dwell on it; you don't have time for that. The game is going on with or without you, and you have to jump on the mental toughness train before it takes off. Find a way to move forward. The thought is simple, but the action takes practice and heart. Bringing 100% to the next pitch and being mentally "all there" for your team has to trump the mistake made. With that said, when trying to improve from errors, use constructive criticism instead of being critical. Two very different ideas where one can help the pitcher rise above negative thoughts. Using constructive criticism allows the pitcher to think about what it takes to move on from the errors, whereas critical thinking consumes what went wrong. Pitchers should use constructive criticism to find fast, effective answers in the game that will allow them to get back out on the mound and back to their best. Always keep goals in mind so as a pitcher you have something to strive for. This idea also gives the pitcher's focus directed away from negativity.

Achieving mental toughness takes a pitcher to the next level. It's important to keep in mind that every pitcher is different and finding the right kind of mental toughness strategies for each one will take experimenting. Practicing mental toughness will give pitchers the opportunity to discover who they are as mentally tough young women. As a pitcher, remaining mentally tough throughout the game sends a message to your teammates and the other team that giving up will never be an option. Learning mental toughness in softball can also transfer to life away from the field. Mental toughness is a gift learned from a great sport that can improve you as an athlete and a person. Build mental toughness, build character, build passion, and bring it.

About Shannon Murray

Shannon Murray is originally from Lawrenceville, Georgia, Shannon graduated in June 2013 from Lawrence University in Appleton, WI. She played four years as a starting pitcher and utility player for the Vikings. She is now an Assistant Coach at Lake Forest College in Lake Forest, IL. Going on 9 years of coaching experience, this is her first position at the collegiate level. She plans on coaching for many years to come and give back to the sport that gave so much to her. Shannon's ultimate goal is to teach her players that they are astounding young women with the potential to be great softball players through hard work, dedication and sacrifice.

Dr. Sherry Werner

"10 Medically- and Scientifically-Based DOs and DON'Ts for Windmill Pitchers"

i.   **DON'T** believe that the windmill pitch is safe and natural. **DO** know that the windmill pitch puts as much stress on the shoulder and elbow joints as professional baseball pitchers.

Studies have been published on baseball and softball pitching that indicate that both types of pitching cause a "pull" on the upper arm (directed toward the elbow) of, on average, 100% body weight.

ii. **DON'T** throw more than 100 pitches in a workout. **DO** have a purpose for each repetition in a pitching workout.

The tiny muscles in the arm that contribute most to windmill pitching fatigue quickly and are at risk for overuse injuries. For this reason, be smart when developing pitching workouts. Have a goal in mind for each drill/pitch in a pitching workout, and, once the goals are met, the workout is over.

iii. **DON'T** forget that pitching, hitting and throwing are very similar movement patterns and utilize the same muscles groups. **DO** remember that it's the combination of pitching, hitting and throwing repetitions that determine the amount of stress placed on the body in any one softball practice.

When planning a softball practice, factor in the total number of repetitions required for each member of the team. The number of non-pitching repetitions required of a windmill pitcher, particularly in a practice setting, is often overlooked. Muscle fatigue leads to diminished performance and increased risk of injury.

iv. **DON'T** forget that a large percentage of athletic performance is the mental side of the game. **DO** remember female athletes, and thus, windmill pitchers have different requirements for maximizing their mental game as compared to male athletes.

*In the words of legendary softball coach, Mike Candrea, "A **male** athlete needs to perform well to feel good about himself, and a **female** athlete needs to feel good about herself in order to perform well."*

v. **DON'T** carry out strength/speed/agility/quickness workouts before pitching workouts. **DO**, if you must carry out strength/speed/ agility/quickness workouts on pitching days, save them for after the pitching portion of the workout.

The muscles used in pitching need to be "fresh" in order for the pitching workout to be beneficial. Any time an athlete pitches a ball her body needs to be as close as possible to be able to go at 100% potential. Long practices are typically counterproductive in this sense.

vi. **DON'T** encourage a windmill pitcher to "slow down and throw strikes." **DO** encourage a windmill pitcher to perform each pitch at max speed.

The windmill pitch happens in less than ½ of 1 second. For this reason, windmill pitching has to be learned and trained "all out," every pitch. Asking an athlete to slow down any movement pattern introduces altered mechanics which ultimately slows down the learning process.

vii. **DON'T** encourage a short stride. **DO** encourage the longest stride possible without giving up the ability to quickly open and close the hips.

Studies have been published on throwing activities, including windmill pitching, indicating that a longer stride is associated with higher ball speeds.

viii. **DON'T** leave the hips open at the instant of ball release. **DO** close the hips to approximately 45 degrees (half-way open and half-way closed) at the instant of ball release.

Studies have been published on the windmill pitch indicating that more stress is placed on the throwing shoulder when the hips are open at release. Pitchers should open and close the hips as quickly as possible.

ix. **DON'T** train windmill pitchers as football players in the weight room. **DO** be sport- and pitching-specific in the weight room.

Emphasis should be place on the back side of the shoulder, core and legs in order to be sport-specific. Pitching, hitting and throwing are all repetitive "pushing" activities and, therefore, "pulling" muscles should be targeted as part of a windmill pitcher's strength program.

x. **DON'T** max out in the weight room during softball season. **DO** be strategic in building a strength base for windmill pitchers during the appropriate portions of the off-season workout program.

Softball is a power sport, meaning quick bursts of muscular activity are important. Maxing out, or taking a muscle group to failure, does not make sense if you want the softball pitcher to perform at her peak performance level on the field.

About Dr. Sherry Werner

Dr. Sherry Werner, PhD is currently a biomechanics consultant with Ben Hogan Sports Medicine, TMI Sports Medicine and Tulane Institute of Sports Medicine and a pitching instructor at the Sherry Werner Fastpitch Academy in the Red Barn Sports Academy. She received a MS degree in Biomechanics from Indiana University in 1989 and a PhD in Biomechanics from The Pennsylvania State University in 1995. She was selected to the COSIDA Academic All-American Softball Team while earning a bachelors degree from Slippery Rock University.

Dr. Werner's research has focused on the effects of throwing motions at the shoulder, elbow and wrist. Sherry released an instructional pitching DVD with Jennie Finch in 2011 and a second in 2013. Sherry's approach, which focuses on maximizing performance while avoiding injury, is based on twenty years of biomechanical study and experience with pitchers at all levels, from professional and Olympic athletes to high school and recreational players. Her instructional techniques include high-speed, frame-by-frame analysis of an athlete's pitching motion. She also teaches pitching clinics and camps, provides coaches' education, and offers sport-specific strength, speed and agility training.

Stacie Mahoe

"How to put in Extra Work that Makes a Difference"

Most great softball players put in some kind of extra work in away from practice. You've probably heard stories of girls spending hours upon hours in the batting cages, extra hours throwing in their backyard, even more hours spent in the gym, and so on and so forth. After all, when you want superior results, you must go the extra mile. You must be willing to do what other players refuse to do. Unfortunately, many players (and their parents/coaches) don't maximize the extra work put in. They focus on the wrong areas and often ask questions such as:

- What conditioning program should we use?

- How much extra time should be put in each week?

- Should we focus more on hitting, fielding, or speed training?

One parent asked me for advice about their daughter's attitude during extra training sessions. Apparently, their daughter clashes with them during these practice sessions. You may be able to relate. I sure can!

This parent stated, *"The problem is her attitude when I help her. She gets frustrated with me, especially when she doesn't hit the ball well during hitting drills. Please help."*

Honest to goodness my first question was, "Are you sure it's your *daughter's* attitude that's the problem?"

I'm not just being a smart-butt with this question! Don't dismiss it. It's a sincere and valid question.

When you see unwanted behavior in your children, try taking a closer look at yourself. So often, a simple change in *YOUR* behavior and attitude effectively sparks the change you want to see in your child. Sometimes that's a tough pill to swallow, but well worth the effort.

In addition...

- Is your child asking you for help outside of practice time?

- What exactly causes her frustration with you?

Perhaps if you eliminate that source of her frustration, her negative attitude will disappear along with it.

I'll be honest, around 12U I stopped coaching my daughter. Just about any coach or instructor who's been in the parent/coach role will tell you that players take instruction from other people much better than they take it from their own parents. If you try to help, it's irritating. If someone else delivers the message, it's gospel.

As one parent put it, "*I am a pitching and hitting instructor. Over the last 15 years I have coached hundreds of girls, including my daughter. Only one player ever seriously doubted my ability. Care to guess which one?*"

It's a very natural part of development for a child to seek out independence from their parents. This is why toddlers insist upon doing tasks "all by myself". This is why teens tend to push so hard against anything that feels even remotely like you are imposing your wishes on their lives. This isn't necessarily a bad thing! It just makes coaching your own child tricky.

This is part of why we allowed our daughter to be coached by others. It benefited us all! She knew she could come to me with questions any time she wanted, but I stopped being her main source of softball instruction. Not only did this reduce conflict between us, but it also gave her the opportunity to experience different coaching styles, different drills, different philosophies, and different softball systems and strategies. Playing for different coaches gave our daughter a greater pool of knowledge from which to learn and grow. This made it even easier for her to find what worked best for her.

When she started high school, she attended the school where I am the assistant coach which made me her coach again. Thankfully, I work more with infielders and she played outfield so we weren't always in each other's hair.

In addition, I typically let other coaches give her feedback. Just as I would allow any player to receive instruction and feedback via the manner and method that works best for them, I did my best to allow that for my daughter as well.

If my daughter wanted to do extra softball training on her own time, we did our best to make that happen. It was always her choice whether we did extra work. What we worked on and for how long was also her choice.

I was basically only there to hit fungo, feed a tee, or throw some soft toss or front toss. If she asked for input, I gave it. We would also record video clips so she could see what was going on for herself. From there she could make her own adjustments or discuss the issues she saw with me.

Confession: we rarely did these extra softball training sessions.

Our daughter actually spent much more time...

> running cross country

> wrestling one season

> doing P90X/Insanity

> doing CrossFit

> powerlifting, etc...

...all of which provided benefits for softball!

As far as instructors are concerned, we never paid for one either. There really aren't many around where we live.

It's *OKAY* if your daughter doesn't want to do extra batting practice or fielding practice with you on her own time. There are many other things she can do and many other ways she can raise her game.

Some players prefer reading. There a ton of great books on improving performance out there. Others prefer hanging out on YouTube and watching videos. There are many helpful videos on hitting, pitching, throwing, fielding, strength and conditioning, mental training, and other performance boosting concepts. Others simply absorb a great deal through observation. I'm one of those people. I gain great insights just by observing softball games, baseball games, athletes overcoming challenges and adversity, and more.

Surfing promotes balance, core strength, body awareness, conditioning, and much more. Video games are used by surgeons for improving eye-hand coordination. Hey, if it's good enough for surgeons, it's good enough for softball players!

The point is, a player has various ways to get better at what they do; and it doesn't always have to look like softball! Plus, it's typically *FAR* more effective to support your daughter in doing "extra work" *SHE WANTS* to do rather than make her do what you think is best. She will spend more time and be more deeply engaged in an activity she enjoys and wants to do. This will produce a greater "return on investment," vs. something she's "made" to do because someone else thinks it's a good idea.

Personally, since private instructors in our area were limited, I ended up reaching out to instructors and began organizing clinics and camps. Part of the arrangement was that my kids attended for free. I know that's not feasible for everyone. Just keep in mind that there are different ways you can help and support your child to become their best. Be willing to think outside of the box!

Also, this period of youth sports goes by *SO* fast in the grand scheme of things. I know it doesn't always feel like it when you're in the thick of it, but one day, it'll be all over. I encourage you to spend more time enjoying what your daughter *IS* doing instead of constantly harping on and being dissatisfied with all of the things you think they should be doing. Your daughter will thrive under your unwavering acceptance, support, and love than under constant scrutiny and criticism. You don't have to be a mean sports parent to be a great one; the game provides enough adversity without you adding to it! Provide the foundation of strength and courage your daughter needs to succeed both in sports and in life.

About Stacie Mahoe

Stacie fell in love with fastpitch softball as a player at the age of 9 and enjoys developing and empowering true champions on and off the field. Find her unique insights, developed through years as a player, coach, and parent, on her blog at www.StacieMahoe.com

Venus Taylor

"Creating the Championship Culture"

I have been both privileged and honored to play and coach the game of softball for over twenty years. I consider coaching to be one of the greatest rewards in life next to being a mother. As a coach you have the chance to make a difference in the lives of your players. You are also given the opportunity to inspire, empower and shape young minds in a positive way that will last beyond your coaching career.

What does that look like? What is the process? What defines success? Do you know your mission as well as your purpose? It is our duty as coaches to lead. We must pay attention to details while creating a process through preparation that will instill confidence in our players, build trust amongst a team and create a championship culture.

A champion is defined as a fighter; a victor in challenge, contest or competition; a person or team who has surpassed all rivals. A championship culture is considered to be the makeup of the player's behavior patterns, thoughts and beliefs. In order to influence and shape a winning culture, you must first decide what building blocks will define your culture.

As a longtime coach and student of the game, I have discussed with my peers our thoughts on what it takes to create a championship culture. I believe there are several core principles to the foundation including:

- Commitment
- Accountability

- Respect
- Trust
- Compassion
- Perseverance
- Responsibility
- Leadership
- Humility
- Integrity

Those in a championship culture are committed to their mission and purpose. Once your team defines their goals, they have to choose to focus on them like a laser beam. As a coach you have to teach your players to see the big picture and explain to them that they are a part of something bigger than themselves. There is no room for selfishness when you make a commitment to a TEAM!

Commitment is daily. You do not have the option to come to practice and say your tired and that you are only going to give 75% today. No excuses! Your personal best is required every single day; you have to rise above the distractions and excuses. Your personal best may change due to illness, injury etc. As an athlete, you have to make the choice that no matter what condition you are in or what struggles you are facing, you will give your best daily and fulfill your commitment to the team mission.

I have always told my players if you can face your teammates and say that you gave your absolute best today, you will not have any regrets. Your best is enough and all that anyone can ask of you. We are always in control of our attitude and our effort. When I recruit players, I look for players who are physically gifted as well as players who show their character through hustle, hard work, good attitude, perseverance and overall effort.

Every team should define their goals at the beginning of the year. The coach should review the goals and determine if they are realistic and attainable. Once you have written and outlined the team goals you must then hold your players accountable to those goals.

I believe in setting a very high standard for the team in which both the players and coaches put an emphasis on work ethic, results, and a way of treating each other. If I see players who are not staying focused or who are being lazy by choice, I will first call them over and ask them if their actions are in line with our mission and our team goals? Most players will tell you no and go back out and work harder. In doing this you are giving the athlete a second chance, teaching them to be accountable, and reminding them what we are working towards as a team. Sometimes players have to be reminded of the process.; the process is continuous. Everything you do leads up to the final moments in which you desire to win a championship.

That being said, if you are going to be at the helm you have to bring it daily as well. You have to be a good example for your team to follow. Actions always speak louder than words.

If your players cannot stay committed to the mission and the goals, then you do not have complete "buy in". You will not sustain a winning culture. If you see anyone off track to the task at hand or ultimate goal then you have to act on it immediately. If the warning does not work, there is always a consequence that will. I do not believe in punishment for errors. I believe in consequences for lack of effort and selfishness. If you let players go through the motions without consequence then you will continue to see them give less than full effort.

I demand perfect effort. You do not have to perform perfectly. We are all human - errors are a part of the game. It makes me cringe when I see travel ball coaches who take their players out every time they make an error. Do you see that happen on television when you watch MLB games? No! Even the best players in the world will make errors. There is no one on the field that will feel worse or more self-aware than the player who made the error.

Respect. Do you treat people the way you wish to be treated? Do you treat yourself, family, teammates, coaches, and officials with respect? I love this topic for so many reasons. Some people are simply not aware of their disrespect while others choose to be arrogant and act as if they are superior. Respect within a championship culture is necessary.

If you have ever played the game before and made a physical error as a player, how would you want your coach to handle it? Do you want them screaming and yelling at you and tearing you down? Does that really keep the player from making an error again? Does it devalue the player and publicly humiliate them on the field? You need to be thinking about these things as a coach because how the players feel is vital to the team's overall success. My suggestion is to provide your players with a positive-critique-positive statement. I find that it works very well. The player gets the information they need to improve while you continue to show them you believe in them and build their confidence.

We have all seen pitchers on the mound who do not get a call their way and roll their eyes for the whole park to see. NO, NO, NO! As a coach, we ask our pitchers, as well as our position players, to be composed. We ask them not to show negative emotion. If you ask your players to exercise control then you have to be able to reciprocate what you are asking of them. For example, do not freak out on umpires and disrespect the officials over a lousy call. Umpires are human too and make mistakes just like the players!

Above all, honor the game and keep it classy. Coaches are not perfect either. We have a sincere passion for the game that runs deep in our veins. Inside of us lies a true competitor in every sense of the word, but we must learn to control our emotions just as we ask our players to control theirs.

I recently had to circle my team up because I noticed a few of the upper classmen yelling at the underclassmen for making errors. It bothered me because I felt as if the upperclassmen had forgotten that they make errors too. The intention of the upperclassmen was to lead. I saw it as creating a divide within the team and being disrespectful to their teammates. I took the time to communicate and address this matter to the team the way I was seeing it. They immediately apologized to each other and left the huddle knowing that there is a better way to lead. It isn't always what you say - it is how you say it. As coaches and teammates, our ultimate goal is to pick each other up and have each other's back through the good times and even more importantly through the bad times.

Trust is a firm belief in the reliability, truth, ability, or strength of someone or something. As a coach, you work hard to get players to "trust" in the process. You have to earn your players trust through your knowledge, reliability and relationship building. Once your players know you care, you will gain their trust and respect.

It is also important to build trust within your staff. Please do not be a control freak! The reason you hire assistant coaches is because they possess a special skill set. You have to give them the freedom to shine and to contribute their strengths to the team. I once read a book by Pat Summit and Pat believes in hiring people who are better then her. I am not sure there were many better than Pat, however, I admire the fact that she is not insecure. Her desire to lead is focused on finding the best coaches to assist her in coaching her team while simultaneously trusting in her own abilities. Pat is a perfect example of coaching with confidence and what confidence at the top can do to lift a team to greatness.

One of my greatest compliments as a coach came from a player from the opposing team. We were playing a very close conference game and I was coaching third base. I believed in my players and I continued to coach them up at third base with positive feedback while they continued to battle at the plate, hoping to string together a couple of hits and win the game. We ended up winning the game and the opposing player walked up to me as I was walking to the vehicle and she said, "I wish I played for a coach like you who believes in her players as much as you do".

I have never forgotten that because in that moment, I realized how important it is to show your players you believe in them when they are in the fight. One of my favorite quotes from Muhammed Ali is, "I am the greatest, I said that before I ever knew I was". Everything starts with a belief. When your players doubt themselves you have to encourage them through positive energy and inspiring words to keep them believing.

Softball is not an easy sport. You fail far more than you succeed. This is one reason why I have so much respect for the players who choose to play baseball and softball.

I have compassion for my athletes because I know what it is like to strike out on that rise ball above my hands because it looked so good coming in. I know what it is like to rip the cover off the ball and have to go back to the dugout because someone made a great catch. I know what it is like to work hard every single day and put in thousands of reps and go 0 for 12 or 0 for 20. The players need to know you have been there. They need to know you know what that feels like and just like you didn't give up on yourself, show them you will never give up on them. You have to show your players you believe in them. Treat your players like you would want another coach to treat your children.

Perseverance is the name of the game both in softball and in life. I once heard a saying that the floor is no place for a champion. That stuck with me. In life and in sports we will get knocked down. We will fail. It is inevitable. You have to refuse to stay there. As a champion, you have to get back up, dust yourself off and keep going. Resilience is an essential trait of a winner.

My favorite athlete of all time is Michael Jordan. Where would he have ended up if he gave up on himself when he was cut from the team? Rule number one in my book is NEVER GIVE UP ON YOURSELF.

Michael Jordan once said, "I've missed more than 9,000 shots in my career. I've lost almost 300 games. 26 times, I've been trusted to take the game winning shot and missed. I've failed over and over again in my life. And that is why I succeed". Michael Jordan may have missed several game winning shots; however, he is remembered for the game winning shots he made due to his ability to persevere and continue to take the shot.

As a coach and as a player you have to know and accept your role. It is the responsibility of the coach to be prepared. As legendary coach John Wooden once said, "Failing to prepare is preparing to fail". Make sure you spend time on building a winning culture. Make sure you have a process and an action plan to help your team reach their daily goals as well as their end goals.

If you want your team to be mentally tough under pressure you must practice the execution of extraordinary excellence. I consider this the "IT" factor. Your players will be more likely to perform in pressure situations in the game if you create a practice plan that entails every pressure situation that will foreseeably arise in the game.

I have always been a coach whose motto is practice like you play. All of my players know I demand adherence to high standards and execution every time they step onto the playing field. I want the players to know and understand that every role on the team is important. I want them to place significant value on every detail of the process. I want the players to celebrate the little things because it really isn't a little thing when you have the right mindset. I push players past their comfort zone because they can't yet see what they are fully capable of doing.

It is important to teach your players to be selfless. It is everyone's work that contributes to the culture. When you truly put the mission and all of your teammates before yourself, you are wholeheartedly committed to the TEAM. Teamwork makes the dream work!

I am a big believer that you have to stay humble. Find gratitude in the simple things. I wake up grateful for the opportunity to wake up. I am grateful to be healthy enough to coach young athletes and give back to the next generation. It is my honor to give back to the game that has given so much to me. I get to do what I love!

We have all been given the blessing of life. I always advise people "pick your passion." Follow your heart. I chose coaching because I feel it is my calling to empower and strengthen young women to go out on the field and into the real world and lead. As a coach, you get the opportunity to sacrifice yourself for the greater good of someone else. I find coaching rewarding because you get to play a small part in creating positive memories, making others dreams come true, and helping equip your players for success in everything they do in life.

Lastly, I would like to stress the importance of having integrity in all you do. It is important for a coach to first and foremost be a good person. You should possess strong moral principles. Be a person of your word. Stand for what you believe in. Do what you say and say what you do. People will like you and respect you when you hold a high standard of integrity. Relationships are everything!

Best Wishes!

About Venus Taylor

Venus Taylor had the unique opportunity to both coach and play at the collegiate and professional levels. Taylor spent her collegiate playing career at Western Illinois University, where she was named Female Athlete of the Year in 1997 and was inducted into the WIU Hall of Fame in 2009. She holds the WIU softball records for hits, stolen bases, and runs scored. After graduating, Venus continued her career in the Women's Professional Softball league for 7 years, being named an all-star 3 times. She was a part of 2 championship teams: the 1999 Tampa Bay Firestix and the 2002 New York/New Jersey Juggernauts. Her coaching career began in her professional off-season with Lake City Community College, where she led the team to a NJCAA championship in 2001. She continued her career at

Georgia Tech, helping the team reach the NCAA Regionals in 2003. In 2011, Venus had the opportunity to serve as an assistant coach with the NPF Chicago Bandits. Taylor's career has not only been on a softball field; from 2006-2011 she served as Wilson Sporting Goods' Fastpitch Business Manager. Currently, she runs Taylor Made Softball where she aids in the development and encouragement of young female athletes.

Bonus Chapter

"30 More Great Tips"

Name: Matt Lisle
Website: www.coachlisle.com **Twitter:** @CoachLisle

Tip: The worst thing a coach can do is develop a philosophy and spend their entire career defending that philosophy.

Name: Dianne I Baker, Hall Of Fame Member
Website: www.schuttsports.com

Tip: Always be trustful with your players from the start. If they are not playing up to expectations, let them know; if you are proud of them, tell them. Players can see right through your words. Be consistent and fair to all.

Name: Danielle Henderson, Former Olympian
Twitter: @danihenderson44

Tip: You should spend every day invested in making every player the best she can be and trying to make them a little bit better than they were the day before. The more you invest in them, the more they will give back to the program.

Name: Jan Greenhawk
Website: www.marylandmagicwagners.com

Tip: It's important that all players, coaches, and parents know the goals of the team, the rules and procedures, and the expectations of every participant. Publish it in writing and get parents and players to sign a copy of it for you to keep and give them a copy. In doing so, you at least assure yourself and everyone else that not only will you be consistent with these rules and procedures, but that parents have a reference and proof that they read and agreed to these rules and procedures in case there is problem. Communication is key!

Name: John Cookson
Website: www.heybucket.com/splash.php **Twitter:** @Heybucket04

Tip: Treat all players the same; you must be consistent. Leave every practice or game on a positive note and be 75% positive and 25% constructive criticism. Don't think as a coach that you cannot learn as well. Make practices fun and mix it up. No one likes to do the same thing old thing all of the time. You need to have a good imagination to keep the players loving the game.

Name: Shannon McDougall
Website: www.softballtutor.com
Twitter: @softballtutor

Tip: Coaches need to include their athletes in the process. Too often, athletes are simply following orders which is fine in the short term; however, it does not promote ownership of the team which will go much further in our quest for a hard working team that never gives up.

Name: Heath Sidaway

Tip: Communication is key between coaches and players regardless of their level of play. If they have been successful, make sure to express that point; if they have been in a slump, chances are they already know, so coaches do not have to drive that point home. Instead, they should be a resource in getting the player out of that slump. Yelling and talking down to players is NOT coaching. Bring them aside and talk to them, they made that team for a reason. Each player has talent and it is your job to help them showcase their abilities.

Name: Cheri Naudin
Website: www.softballacademyoftexas.com **Twitter:** @CheriNaudin

Tip: Teach them to THINK. When you teach them the ins and outs of the game and teach them to think, it goes farther then trying to tell them what to do each time the ball is hit. Praise each kid each game for the best things that they do. Encourage them to be their best and to have fun while competing. Reward the "excellence" that each kid has to offer. Teach and train during pre-game and practices. Contain your frustrations on and off the field as everyone is watching. Being a coach is more than teaching them the game of softball because you are a role model and everything you do is an example for them on and off of the field. Think about the impact everything you do will have on kids and their future.

Name: Dana Maggs
Website: www.facebook.com/pages/Excel-Hitting-And-Pitching/200319390007653
Twitter: @Excel_H_and_P

Tip: When hitting you should track the ball in with the eyes and then at contact the head should not move. It needs to remain still. Too many hitters like to admire their work and will move their heads during and after contact. You will not make solid contact with the ball if you do this and you will strike out more often. Probably the single biggest issue I work on with my hitting students once the absolutes of the swing have been established.

Name: Kate Modrovsky
Twitter: @redstormkate12

Tip: Put away the cookie cutter! There are many different ways to achieve a desired performance result. Help your athlete find what works for her, even if it seems unorthodox. If she is comfortable with her set up and mechanics, she will perform at her absolute best.

Name: Mike Tully
Website: coachtully@totalgameplan.com **Twitter:** @TotalGamePlan

Tip: Work on what you are working on while you're working on it. Before starting the drill, decide what aspect of the skill you must improve. Then practice the aspect you've identified. Don't get distracted by results. Concentrate on the process. Remember: Work on what you are working on while you're working on it.

Name: Shawna May

Tip: Strive for perfection, even though there is no such thing in the game of life or softball. If you're goal is to obtain perfection, then you will always be the perfect player and teammate. When you stop chasing perfection, another player is achieving it.

Name: Scott Knight
Website: www.thundersoftballfamily.com **Twitter:** @mythundergirls

Tip: Repetition...Repetition...Repetition - You can either give your players 100 fly balls, grounders, and swings per practice or you can give them a thousand. Keep it moving and give them thousands of reps per practice!

Name: Sam Banister

Tip: Get to know each of your players on a personal level. Each one has a different story and a different way of learning. If your players know (feel it in their bones) that you're invested in them and their personal growth, they'll go to battle for you every day without hesitation

Name: William Knoppi
Website: www.usssawa.com **Twitter:** @wausssafp

Tip: Knowing how and when to protest. Weather it is an inexperienced official, one that works multiple sanctions, just forgot the rule, or does not know it. The way rules are implemented will impact the game. Ask for time. Get the explanation and if you think the rule is not being properly used then notify the umpire you are protesting the game and it there is a UIC and ask for the UIC.

Name: Michele Granger, Former Olympian

Tip: The hard work and repetition of practice is only one part of building a successful team the tougher piece to the puzzle is getting your athletes to push themselves to always play at 100 percent effort and to play with no fear of failure.

Name: Jen Croneberger
Website: www.thefivewords.com **Twitter:** @JenCroneberger

Tip: From head to toe, teams can be tricky to navigate. A mix of personalities and agendas can make team-building a mighty feat and it is a task that is not for the faint of heart. It can also be a completely beautiful yet complex process of discovery.

I have spent countless hours with teams of all shapes and sizes, from sports to schools to corporations to musicians, all with one goal in mind: to come together surrounding their specific mission, whatever that was. To realize a goal with many different people involved is difficult and the only way to really get past survival mode is to learn how to thrive together. That takes a special effort and a lot of patience and understanding. None of that can ever take place without first surrounding oneself with awareness.

Breaking down the anatomy of a team seems simple at first, but all of the moving parts have a place, and if they are not pieced together properly the puzzle will always be unfinished.

Name: Ryan Harrison
Website: www.SlowTheGameDown.com **Twitter:**@SlowTheGameDown

Tip: The visual side of the game is invisible to an observer, but the player knows that when he sees the ball well he is confident and capable of hitting, throwing, or fielding effectively. Ask questions. Don't just assume it is a physical or mental mistake. Everything a player does on the playing field begins with what he sees or a visual thought and ends with what he sees.
Ask the players what are they looking at/for.
What are they focused on preceding the time of action?
What are they focused on at the time of action?
What are they focused on after the time of action?

Name: Danny Gershwin

Tip: I see too many young coaches that work with younger girls telling them to be aggressive, yet criticize them when they make mistakes when they are aggressive. The result, more often than not, are girls that are passive or robotic. If you're willing to put up with a few mistakes at the outset and compliment them instead of criticize, you'll be rewarded in the long run.

Name: Robby Wilson, NSR Softball Director
Website: www.nsr-inc.com/softball **Twitter:** @robbywilsonnsr

Tip: Think of each individual athlete, and at the end, it will benefit the team as a whole. Don't schedule showcases and tournaments every single weekend. Give them equal weekends off where the players can attend camps they were invited to, can go on unofficial visits, or even simply to have a weekend to be a kid! Don't carry 25 on a travel roster; 12-14 is plenty. Girls understand competition is healthy, but sitting too much is unhealthy. Being gone every weekend to play, then only playing 4 innings out of 5 games, it's no wonder we see so much "burn out" from such high caliber players. Let's get back to the basics: play every other weekend; 12-14 is plenty; have fun and compete. It's better for the team, the individual girl, and better for recruiting.

Name: Rich Hoppe, pitcher, THE KING AND HIS COURT

Tip: A poster on a phone pole in 1961 would change my life forever. That night I saw The King and his Court, 6,500games, events, exhibitions, 44 countries, from major league stadiums, legendary softball arenas, prisons, military bases, 47 summers(170-215cities each spring to fall). Nn 2011, labor day weekend, Walla Walla, Wa. in front of a packed house, where it all began, we said goodbye and a mighty thanks for all the 65yrs we toured the world. "DREAMS COME TRUE", WHERE I FOUND SELF AND SOUL"

Name: Stacey Nelson
Tip: Only look forward. The next pitch is always the most important.

Name: Alan Jaeger
Website: jaegersoftball.com & jaegersports.com **Twitter:** @jaegersports

Tip: The 2 most neglected parts of the game are, 1)Mental Practice, and 2) Arm Care/Arm Development. Attention to these parts of the game may have the single most dramatic impact regarding the development of your players.

Name: Darren Darracq
Website: www.dfwfastpitch.info **Twitter:** @DFWfastpitch

Tip: Girls should be trained to cover the advancing base and hand or flip the ball to pitcher after base runner gets on base. Do not make unnecessary throws that may advance runners.

Name: Leah Amico, Former Olympian
Website: www.leah20.com **Twitter:** @leah20usa

Tip: Confidence is crucial for athletes to be successful. A coach that is process oriented rather than outcome oriented allows players to build confidence and understand that preparation will lead to success. When a coach and a player can find the positive in a hard hit ground ball or a line drive to the opposite side of the field, regardless of the outcome, confidence grows for the next opportunity. The best coaches help players to focus on what they can control and to have quality at bats or good defensive mechanics and build on that foundation. When players don't have pressure on results for every single play, they can focus on quality at-bats and begin to trust that success will follow with solid contact and hitting their pitch. Ultimately this builds confidence in a player and every successful athlete rises to the top when they are confident. The key is for the coach to verbalize this focus on the process and the players will follow along with that same focus.

Name: Marc Dagenais
Website: SoftballPerformance.com **Twitter:** @coachmarc

Tip: Take your warm-up seriously. The quality of your warm-up will often dictate the quality of your performance. It helps your prepare not only physically but mentally as well. Develop a specific warm-up routine for your workouts, your practices and your games. This will help you perform to your best!

Name: Bill Boles

Tip: Softball is not a game of perfect, a coach should have the ability to mentor kids to play according to the bar they set for themselves. It is the responsibility of the coach to help them set achievable and measurable goals so that they can eliminate self doubt, and celebrate their accomplishments. Girls know when they make mistakes and errors, and they are hard on themselves because they want to please their teammates, coaches and parents. They should be taught to play and compete at a level according to the roadmap they have established for themselves and all the people in the background will support their effort.

Name: Phoenix Strange (age 7)

Tip: Make sure to have fun. It's not all about winning, it's about having fun. When I played soccer, I thought it was all about winning but then I realized there was no scoreboard, so it was really about having fun.

Resources

Over the years, I have developed a large network of websites dedicated to Girls Fastpitch Softball.

Some are educational, while some have my softball ecommerce sites.

I thought I would share them with you here:

www.Fastpitch.TV

www.FastpitchMagazine.com

www.SportsJunk.com

www.SoftballJunk.com

www.SoftballStuff.com

www.USAfastpitch.com

www.SoftballCoaches.com

www.FastpitchFlowers.com

www.WeightedBalls.com

www.BaseCoachHelmets.com

www.BaseballJunk.com

www.FaceGuards.com

www.BatTape.com

www.EyeblackStickers.com

www.StrikeZoneMat.com

www.WindmillTrainer.com

www.CatchersZone.com

www.BuntSock.com

www.MiniHelmets.com

www.SportsDecorating.com

I Produce Fastpitch Video & Audio Podcasts:

Find The Show Links at - www.Fastpitch.TV/Podcasts

The Names of My Podcasts Are:

The Fastpitch Softball TV Show

Fastpitch Radio

Fastpitch Chat Show

Softball Stuff Show

Conclusion

I hope you found these questions and answers helpful. If you would like to receive my free newsletter, sign up at:

Fastpitch.TV/Newsletter

Best Regards,

Gary Leland

Made in the USA
San Bernardino, CA
24 April 2016